BARMANS' A-Z GUIDE TO
COCKTAILS

R&R PUBLICATIONS MARKETING PTY LTD

Published by:
R&R Publications Marketing Pty. Ltd
12 Edward Street'
Brunswick, Victoria 3054
Australia
Australia wide toll free 1 800 063 296
E-mail: info@randrpublications.com.au
Web: www.randrpublications.com.au
©Richard Carroll

Publisher: Richard Carroll
Mixed Drinks Research: Jon Carroll
Creative Director: Paul Sims
Project Manager: Anthony Carroll
Photography: Warren Webb
Presentation: Jon Carroll
Photography Assistance: Samatha Carroll

The National Library of Australia
Cataloguing-in-Publication Data
The complete book of mixed drinks.
Includes index.
ISBN: 1 74022 266 0
EAN: 9 781740 222662

1. Cocktails. 2. Beverages. 3. Alcoholic beverages.

This edition printed September 2003

Computer Typeset in ITC Eras and Palatino
Printed in Singapore by Saik Wah Press Pte Ltd

Table of Contents

Introduction

METHODS OF MIXING COCKTAILS

The four methods below are the most common processes of mixing cocktails:-

1. Shake   **2.** Stir

3. Build   **4.** Blend

1. SHAKE: To shake is to mix a cocktail by shaking it in a cocktail shaker by hand. First, fill the glass part of the shaker three quarters full with ice, then pour the ingredients on top of the ice. Less expensive ingredients are more frequently poured before the deluxe ingredients. Pour the contents of the glass into the metal part of the shaker and shake vigorously for ten to fifteen seconds. Remove the glass section and using a Hawthorn strainer, strain contents into the cocktail glass. Shaking ingredients that do not mix easily with spirits is easy and practical (juices, egg whites, cream and sugar syrups).

Most shakers have two or three parts. In a busy bar, the cap is often temporarily misplaced. If this happens, a coaster or the inside palm of your hand is quite effective. American shakers are best.

To sample the cocktail before serving to the customer, pour a small amount into the shaker cap and using a straw check the taste.

2. STIR: To stir a cocktail is to mix the ingredients by stirring them with ice in a mixing glass and then straining them into a chilled cocktail glass. Short circular twirls are most preferred. (NB. The glass part of the American shaker will do well for this.) Spirits, liqueurs and vermouths that blend easily together are mixed by this method.

3. BUILD: To build a cocktail is to mix the ingredients in the glass in which the cocktail is to be served, floating one on top of the other. Hi-Ball, long fruit juice and carbonated mixed cocktails are typically built using this technique. Where possible a swizzle stick should be put into the drink to mix the ingredients after being presented to the customer. Long straws are excellent substitutes when swizzle sticks are unavailable.

4. BLEND: To blend a cocktail is to mix the ingredients using an electric blender/mixer. It is recommended to add the fruit (fresh or tinned) first. Slicing small pieces gives a smoother texture than if you add the whole fruit. Next, pour the alcohol. Ice should always be added last. This order ensures that the fruit is blended freely with the alcoholic ingredients allowing the ice to gradually mix into the food and beverage, chilling the flavour. Ideally, the blender should be on for at least 20 seconds. Following this procedure will prevent ice and fruit lumps that then need to be strained.

If the blender starts to rattle and hum, ice may be obstructing the blades from spinning. Always check that the blender is clean before you start. Angostura Bitters is ammonia based which is suitable for cleaning. Fill 4 to 5 shakes with hot water, rinse and then wipe clean.

TECHNIQUES IN MAKING COCKTAILS

1. SHAKE AND POUR: After shaking the cocktail, pour the contents straight into the glass. When pouring into Hi-Ball glasses and sometimes old fashioned glasses the ice cubes are included. This eliminates straining.

Introduction

2. SHAKE AND STRAIN: Using a Hawthorn strainer (or knife) this technique prevents the ice going into the glass. Straining protects the cocktail ensuring melted ice won't dilute the flavour and mixture.

3. FLOAT INGREDIENTS: Hold the spoon right way up and rest it with the lip slightly above the level of the last layer. Fill spoon gently and the contents will flow smoothly from all around the rim. Use the back of the spoons dish only if you are experienced.

4. FROSTING (sugar and salt rims): This technique is used to coat the rim of the glass with either salt or sugar. First, rub lemon/orange slice juice all the way around only the glass rim. Next, holding the glass by the stem upside down, rest on a plate containing salt or sugar and turn slightly so that it adheres to the glass. Pressing the glass too deeply into the salt or sugar often results in chunks sticking to the glass. A lemon slice is used for salt and an orange slice is used for sugar.

To achieve colour affects, put a small amount of grenadine or coloured liqueur in a plate and coat the rim of the glass, then gently place in the sugar. The grenadine absorbs the sugar and turns it pink. This is much easier than mixing grenadine with sugar and then trying to get it to stick to the glass.

HELPFUL HINTS
Cocktail mixing is an art which is expressed in the preparation and presentation of the cocktail.

HOW TO MAKE A BRANDY ALEXANDER CROSS
Take two short straws and, with a sharp knife, slice one of the straws half way through in the middle and wedge the other uncut straw into the cut straw to create a cross.

STORING FRUIT JUICES
Take a 750ml bottle and soak it in hot water to remove the label and sterilise the alcohol. The glass has excellent appeal and you'll find it easier to pour the correct measurement with an attached nip pourer.

SUGAR SYRUP RECIPE
Fill a cup or bowl (depending on how much you want to make) with white sugar, top it up with boiling water until the receptacle is just about full and keep stirring until the sugar is fully dissolved. Refrigerate when not in use. Putting a teaspoon of sugar into a cocktail is being lazy, it does not do the job properly as the sugar dissolves.

JUICE TIPS
Never leave juices, Coconut Cream or other ingredients in cans. Pour them into clean bottles, cap and refrigerate them. All recipes in this book have been tested with Berri fruit juices.

ICE
Ice is probably the most important part of cocktails. It is used in nearly all cocktails. Consequently ice must be clean and fresh at all times.

The small squared cubes and flat chips of ice are superior for chilling and mixing cocktails. Ice cubes with holes are inefficient. Wet ice, ice scraps and broken ice should only be used in blenders.

Introduction

CRUSHED ICE

Take the required amount of ice and fold into a clean linen cloth. Although uncivilised, the most effective method is to smash it against the bar floor. Shattering with a bottle may break the bottle. Certain retailers sell portable ice crushers. Alternatively a blender may be used. Half fill with ice and then pour water into the blender until it reaches the level of the ice. Blend for about 30 seconds, strain out the water and you have perfectly crushed ice. Always try and use a metal scoop to collect the ice from the ice tray.

Never pick up the ice with your hands. This is unhygienic. Shovelling the glass into the ice tray to gather ice can also cause breakages and hence should be avoided where possible.

It is important that the ice tray is cleaned each day. As ice is colourless and odourless, many people assume wrongly it is always clean. Taking a cloth soaked in hot water, wipe the inside of the bucket warm. The blenders used for all of our bar requirements are Moulinex blenders with glass bowls. We have found these blenders to be of exceptional quality.

GLASSES

Cordial (Embassy):	30mL	Fancy Hi-Ball Glass:	220mL, 350mL, 470mL
Cordial (Lexington):	37mL	Hurricane Glass:	230mL, 440mL, 650mL
Tall Dutch Cordial:	45mL	Irish Coffee Glass:	250mL
Whisky Shot:	45mL	Margarita Glass:	260mL
Martini Glass:	90mL	Hi-Ball Glass:	270mL, 285mL, 330mL
Cocktail Glass:	90mL, 140mL	Footed Hi-Ball Glass:	270mL, 300mL
Champagne Saucer:	140mL	Salud Grande Glass:	290mL
Champagne Flute:	140mL, 180mL	Fiesta Grande Glass:	350mL, 490mL
Wine Goblet:	140mL, 190mL	Poco Grande Glass:	380mL
Old Fashioned Spirit:	185mL, 210mL, 290mL	Brandy Balloon:	650mL
Fancy Cocktail:	210mL, 300mL		

A proven method to cleaning glasses is to hold each glass individually over a bucket of boiling water until the glass becomes steamy and then with a clean linen cloth rub in a circular way to ensure the glass is polished for the next serve

Cocktails can be poured into any glass but the better the glass the better the appearance of the cocktail.

One basic rule should apply and that is, use no coloured glasses as they spoil the appearance of cocktails. All glasses have been designed for a specific task, e.g.,

1. Hi-Ball glasses for long cool refreshing drinks.
2. Cocktail glasses for short sharp, or stronger drinks.
3. Champagne saucers for creamy after-dinner style drinks, etc.,

The stem of the glass has been designed so you may hold it whilst polishing, leaving the bowl free of marks and germs so that you may enjoy your drink. All cocktail glasses should be kept in a refrigerator or filled with ice while you are preparing the cocktails in order to chill the glass. An appealing affect on a 90ml cocktail glass can be achieved by running the glass under cold water and then placing it in the freezer.

GARNISHES AND JUICES

Banana
Celery
Cucumber
Lemons
Limes
Mint leaves
Olives
Celery salt
Chocolate flake
Cinnamon
Fresh eggs
Fresh single cream
Fresh milk
Apple
Carbonated waters
Coconut Cream
Lemon – pure
Orange
Jelly Babies
Almonds
Apricot Conserve
Vanilla Ice Cream

Onions
Oranges
Pineapple
Red Maraschino Cherries
Rockmelon
Strawberries
Canned fruit
Nutmeg
Pepper, Salt
Tomato
Sugar and sugar cubes
Tabasco sauce
Worcestershire sauce
Orange and Mango
Pineapple
Sugar syrup
Canned nectars
Canned pulps
Crushed Pineapple
Blueberries
Red Cocktail Onions
Flowers (assorted)

Simplicity is the most important fact to keep in mind when garnishing cocktails. Do not overdo the garnish; make it striking, but if you can't get near the cocktail to drink it then you have failed. Most world champion cocktails just have a lemon slice, or a single red cherry.

Tall refreshing Hi-Balls tend to have more garnish as the glass is larger. A swizzle stick should be served nearly always in long cocktails. Straws are always served for a lady, but optional for a man.

Plastic animals, umbrellas, fans and a whole variety of novelty goods are now available to garnish with, and they add a lot of fun to the drink.

ALCOHOL RECOMMENDED FOR A COCKTAIL BAR

Spirits

Ouzo
Bourbon
Brandy
Campari
Canadian Club
Gin
Malibu
Pernod
Rum

Scotch
Southern Comfort
Tennessee Whiskey
Tequila
Vandermint
Vodka
S

Introduction

Liqueurs

Advocaat
Amaretto
Bailey's Irish Cream
Banana
Benedictine
Blue Curacao
Cassis
Chartreuse – Green & Yellow
Cherry Advocaat
Cherry Brandy
Clayton's Tonic (Non-alcoholic)
Coconut
Cointreau
Creme de cafe
Creme de Menthe Green
Dark Creme de Cacao
Drambuie

Frangelico
Galliano
Grand Marnier
Kahlúa
Kirsch
Kirsch
Mango
Melon
Orange
Peach
Pimm's
Sambuca – Clear
Sambuca – Black
Strawberry
Triple Sec

Vermouth

Cinzano Bianco Vermouth
Cinzano Dry Vermouth
Cinzano Rosso Vermouth

Martini Bianco Vermouth
Martini Dry Vermouth
Martini Rosso Vermouth

ESSENTIAL EQUIPMENT FOR A COCKTAIL BAR

Cocktail shaker
Hawthorn Strainer
Mixing glass
Spoon with muddler
Moulinex Electric blender
Knife, cutting board
Measures (jiggers)
Can opener
Hand cloths for cleaning glasses

Waiter's friend corkscrew
Bottle openers
Ice scoop
Ice bucket
Free pourers
Swizzle sticks, straws
Coasters and napkins
Scooper spoon (long teaspoon)

DESCRIPTION OF LIQUEURS AND SPIRITS

Advocaat: A combination of fresh egg whites, yolks, sugar, brandy, vanilla and spirit. Limited shelf life, Recommend shelf life 12-15 months from manufacture.

Amaretto: A rich subtle liqueur with a unique almond flavour.

Angostura Bitters: An essential part of any bar or kitchen. A unique additive whose origins date back to 1824. A mysterious blend of natural herbs and spices, both a seasoning and flavouring agent, in both sweet and savoury dishes and drinks. Ideal for dieters as it is low in sodium and calories.

Introduction

Baileys Irish Cream: The largest selling liqueur in the world. sIt is a blend of Irish Whiskey, softened by Irish Cream and other flavourings. It is a natural product.

Banana: Fresh ripe bananas are the perfect base for the definitive daiquiri and a host of other exciting fruit cocktails.

Benedictine: A perfect end to a perfect meal. Serve straight, with ice, soda, or as part of a favourite cocktail.

Bourbon – Has a smooth, deep, easy flavour.

Brandy – Smooth and mild spirit, is considered a very smooth and palatable, ideal for mixing.

Campari: A drink for many occasions, both as a long or short drink, or as a key ingredient in many fashionable cocktails.

Cassis: Deep, rich purple promises and delivers a regal and robust flavour and aroma. Cassis lends itself to neat drinking or an endless array of delicious sauces and desserts.

Chartreuse: A liqueur available in either yellow or green colour. Made by the monks of the Carthusian order. The only world famous liqueur still made by monks.

Cherry Advocaat: Same as Advocaat, plus natural cherry flavours and colour is added.

Cherry Brandy: Is made from concentrated, morello cherry juice. Small quantity of bitter almonds and vanilla is added to make it more enjoyable as a neat drink before or after dinner. Excellent for mixers, topping, ice cream, fruit salads, pancakes, etc.

Coconut: A smooth liqueur, composed of exotic coconut, heightened with light-bodied white rum.

Cointreau: Made from a neutral grain spirit, as opposed to Cognac. An aromatic flavour of natural citrus fruits. A great mixer or delightful over ice.

Creme de Cacao Dark: Rich, deep chocolate. Smooth and classy. Serve on its own, or mix for all kinds of delectable treats.

Creme de Cacao White: This liqueur delivers a powerfully lively, full bodied chocolate flavour. Excellent ingredient when absence of colour is desired.

Creme de Grand Marnier: A blend of Grand Marnier and smooth French cream. A premium product, a very smooth taste with the orange/cognac flavour blending beautifully with smooth cream.

Creme de Menthe Green: Clear peppermint flavour, reminiscent of a fresh, crisp, clean winter's day in the mountains. Excellent mixer, a necessity in the gourmet kitchen.

Creme de Menthe White: As Creme de Menthe Green, when colour is not desired.

Curacao Blue: Same as Triple Sec, brilliant blue colour is added to make some cocktails more exciting.

Curacao Orange: Again, same as above, but stronger in orange, colouring is used for other varieties of cocktail mixers.

Introduction

Curacao Triple Sec: Based on natural citrus fruits. Well known fact is citrus fruits are the most important aromatic flavour constituents. Interesting to know citrus fruit was known 2,000 years before Christ. As a liqueur one of the most versatile. Can be enjoyed with or without ice as a neat drink, or used in mixed cocktails more than any other liqueur. Triple Sec – also known as White Curacao.

Galliano: The distinguished taste! A classic liqueur that blends with a vast array of mixed drinks.

Gin: Its aroma comes from using the highest quality juniper berries and other rare and subtle herbs. Perfect mixer for both short and long drinks.

Kirsch: A fruit brandy distilled from morello cherries. Delicious drunk straight and excellent in a variety of food recipes.

Drambuie: A Scotch whisky liqueur. Made from a secret recipe dating back to 1745. "Dram Buidheach" the drink that satisfies.

Frangelico: A precious liqueur imported from Italy. Made from wild hazelnuts with infusions of berries and flowers to enrich the flavour.

Grand Marnier: An original blend of fine old Cognac and an extract of oranges. The recipe is over 150 years old

Kahlúa: A smooth, dark liqueur made from real coffee and fine clear spirits. Its origins are based in Mexico.

Malibu: A clear liqueur based on white rum with the subtle addition of coconut. Its distinctive taste blends naturally with virtually every mixer available.

Melon Liqueur: Soft green, exudes freshness. Refreshing and mouth-watering honeydew melon. Simple yet complex. Smooth on the palate, serve on the rocks, or use to create summertime cocktails.

Ouzo: The traditional spirit aperitif of Greece. The distinctive flavour is derived mainly from the seed of the anise plant. A neutral grain spirit, flavoured with anise.

Peach: The flavour of fresh peaches and natural peach juice make this cocktail lover's dream.

Peachtree Schnapps: Crystal clear, light liqueur, bursting with the taste of ripe peaches. Drink chilled or on the rocks or mix with any soft drink or juice.

Pineapple: A just ripe, sun-filled delight. Delicious neat, a necessity for summertime cocktails.

Rum: A smooth, dry, light bodied rum, especially suited for drinks in which you require subtle aroma and delicate flavour.

Rye Whiskey: Distilled from corn, rye and malted barley. A light, mild and delicate Whiskey, ideal for drinking straight or in mixed cocktails.

Sabra: A unique flavour which comes from tangy jaffa oranges, with a hint of chocolate.

Introduction

Sambuca – Clear: The Italian electric taste experience. Made from elderberries with a touch of anise.

Sambuca – Black: An exciting encounter between Sambuca di Galliano and extracts of black elderberry.

Scotch Whisky – A blended whisky.

Southern Comfort: A liqueur not a bourbon as often thought. It is unique, full-bodied liquor with a touch of sweetness. Its recipe is a secret, but it is known to be based on peaches and apricots.

Strawberry: Fluorescent red, unmistakable strawberry bouquet. Natural liqueur delivers a true to nature, fresh strawberry flavour.

Tennessee Whiskey : Contrary to popular belief, this is not a bourbon, it is a distinctive product called Tennessee Whiskey. Made from the 'old sour mash' process. Leached through hard maple charcoal, then aged in charred white oak barrels, at a controlled temperature, acquiring its body, bouquet and colour, yet remaining smooth.

Tequila: Distilled from the Mexcal variety of the cacti plant. A perfect mixer or drink straight with salt and lemon.

Tia Maria: A liqueur with a cane spirit base, and its flavour derived from the finest Jamaican coffee. It is not too sweet with a subtle taste of coffee.

Vandermint: A rich chocolate liqueur with the added zest of mint.

Vermouth: By description, Vermouth is a herbally infused wine.

Three styles are most prevalent, these are:

> **Rosso:** A bitter sweet herbal flavour, often drunk as an aperitif.
>
> **Bianco:** Is light, fruity and refreshing. Mixes well with soda, lemonade and fruit juices.
>
> **Dry:** Is crisp, light and dry and is used as a base for many cocktails.

Vodka: The second largest selling spirit in the world. Most Vodkas are steeped in tanks containing charcoal, removing all odours and impurities, making a superior quality product.

Triple Sec: See Blue Curacao.

Aberdeen Angus

Ingredients

Glass: 140mL/5fl oz Cocktail Glass

Mixers: 30mL/1fl oz scotch whisky
10mL/⅓fl oz Drambuie
1 tablespoon honey
10mL/⅓fl oz fresh lime juice

Method

Blend with ice and pour. Garnish with two banana wheel slices wedged on rim of glass.

Acapulco

Ingredients

Glass: 150mL/5fl oz Old Fashioned Glass

Mixers: 30mL/1fl oz Bacardi
10mL/1fl oz Cointreau
1 egg white
15mL/⅓fl oz fresh lime juice
add sugar to taste

Method

Shake over ice and pour. Garnish with partially torn mint leaves.

Alabama Slammer

Ingredients

Glass: Whisky Shot

Mixers: 10 mL/⅓fl oz gin
10 mL/⅓fl oz Amaretto
10 mL/⅓fl oz orange juice
10 mL/½fl oz Southern Comfort

Method

Pour in order then shoot.

A real drink! From the heart of the Deep South, USA.

Alaska

Ingredients

Glass: 130mL/4½ oz Cocktail Glass

Mixers: 30mL/1fl oz gin
               10mL/⅓fl oz Yellow Chartreuse
               1-2 dashes of Orange Curacao

Method

Shake over ice and strain. Garnish with orange twist.

Almond Orange Frost

Ingredients

Glass: 240mL/8oz Champagne
Sherbert Glass

Mixers: 15mL/½fl oz Amaretto
15mL/½fl oz Frangelico
15mL/½fl oz Chambord
10mL/⅓fl oz fresh lime juice
10mL/⅓fl oz fresh lemon juice
1 teaspoon chopped almonds
2 scoops orange sherbert

Method

Blend with ice. Garnish with orange slice and chopped almonds.

Americano

Ingredients

Glass: 270mL/9oz Highball Glass

Mixers: 30mL/1fl oz campari
30mL/1fl oz Cinzano Rosso
Vermouth
top up with soda

Method

Build over ice and top up with soda. Garnish with orange slice.

Comments: Originated from European travellers visiting America desiring a taste of European aperitifs.

Aqua Thunder

Ingredients

Glass: 285mL/10oz Hi-Ball Glass

Mixers: 10mL/⅓fl oz Blue Curacao Liqueur
10mL/⅓fl oz Banana Liqueur
30mL/1fl oz Melon Liqueur
10mL/⅓fl oz freshly squeezed lemon
top-up with soda water

Method

Build over ice.

Garnish: Swizzle stick, and slice of lemon.

Comments: Watch in wonder as the soda waterfall
splashes over the ice creating a thunderous aqua-coloured
spectacular.

Aquavit Fiz

Ingredients

Glass: 170mL/6oz Tulip Champagne Glass

Mixers: 45mL/1½fl oz Aquavit

30mL/1fl oz lemon juice

15mL/½fl oz Cherry Heering

10mL/⅓fl oz sugar syrup

1 egg white

top up with soda

Method

Shake over ice and strain then top up with soda. Garnish
with a red cherry.

ASBSOLUT Cosmopolitan

Ingredients

Glass: 90mL/3oz Martini Glass (chilled)

Mixers: 45mL/1½fl oz ABSOLUT CITRON

20mL/²/₃fl oz Triple Sec Liqueur

20mL/²/₃fl oz Cranberry Classic

juice of ½ fresh lime

Method

Shake with ice and strain into chilled martini glass.

Mixers: With orange twist.

Comments: A citrus tasting masterpiece. A very pleasant cocktail, destined to be a classic.

ASBSOLUT Iceberg

Ingredients

Glass: 285mL/10oz Highball Glass

Mixers: 30mL/1fl oz ABSOLUT CITRON

15mL/¹/₂fl ozfl oz Triple Sec Liqueur

150mL/5fl oz Bitter lemon

Method

Pour ABSOLUT CITRON and Triple Sec over ice into a chilled highball glass and top with Bitter Lemon.

Garnish: Orange slice

Comments: A delightful long citrus drink for a hot day.

Australian Gold

Ingredients

Glass: 90mL/3oz Cocktail Glass

Mixers: 30mL/1fl oz Rum
               30mL/1fl oz Mango Liqueur
               30mL/1fl oz Galliano

Method

Build over ice.

Garnish: 1 small pineapple wedge.

Comments: This straight spirit cocktail is also known as **"Queensland Wine".**

B & B

Ingredients

Glass: Brandy Balloon

Mixers: 30mL/1fl oz Martell Cognac
30mL/1fl oz Benedictine

Method

Build, no ice.

Garnish: None.

Comments: Tempt your pallet with this historical blend of choice liqueurs. Relaxing by the fire on winter nights, the genuine connoisseur will enjoy interesting conversation with friends. Ideal with coffee.

Banana Colada

Ingredients

Glass: 300mL/10oz Fancy Glass

Mixers: 30mL/1fl oz Bacardi
30mL/1fl oz Sugar syrup
30mL/1fl oz Coconut cream
30mL/1fl oz Cream
120m/4fl oz Pineapple juice
$^1/_2$ Banana

Method

Build with ice and pour.

Garnish: Slice of banana, pineapple spear and mint leaves.
Serves with straws.

Comments: A simple exemplary cocktail to demostrate the
variety of fruits available. Be adventurous and surprise
yourself!

Banana Daiquiri

Ingredients

Glass: 140mL/5oz Champagne Saucer

Mixers: ¾ Banana
30mL/1fl oz Sugar syrup
30mL/1fl oz Bacardi
30mL/1fl oz Lemon juice

Method

Blend with ice and strain.

Garnish : Round slice of banana and mint leaves.

Comments : Frequently served on arrival at cocktail parties, this icy cold mixture is always warmly received by guests. Simple to prepare in large quantities, different combinations of fruits can be added to the base mix without deliberation. Adjust measurements of lemon and sugar accordly for a sweeter or sour taste. Where unripe fruit is used, fruit liqueurs will enrich the flavour.

Bananarama

Ingredients

Glass: 140mL/5oz Cocktail Glass

Mixers: 30mL/1fl oz Vodka
30mL/1fl oz Kahlúa
15mL/¹⁄₂fl oz Baileys Irish Cream
1 Banana
60mL/2fl oz Cream

Method

Blend with ice and pour.

Garnish: Two banana wheel slices wedged on rim of glass.

Comments: A delightful cocktail, drunk on the North Queensland island resorts, where tourists dance the "RAMA".

Bemuda Rose

Ingredients

Glass:　　90mL/3oz Cocktail Glass

Mixers:　　30mL/1fl oz gin

10mL/⅓fl oz lime juice

5mL/⅙fl oz Grenadine

4-5 drops of Apricot Brandy

Method

Shake over ice and strain. Garnish with a slice of lime.

Between The Sheets

Ingredients

Glass: 140mL/5oz Champagne Saucer

Mixers: 30mL/1fl oz Brandy
30mL/1fl oz Bacardi
30mL/1fl oz Cointreau
15mL/½fl oz Lemon juice

Method

Shake with ice and strain.

Garnish: Garnish with lemon slice and twist.

Comments: A pre-dinner cocktail. A fine blend of traditional spirits for the mature pallet. It may be served with a lemon twist.

Black Opal

Ingredients

Glass: 90mL/3oz Cocktail Glass

Mixers: 15mL/½fl oz Black Sambuca
                15mL/½fl oz Cointreau
                15mL/½fl oz Baileys Irish Cream
                15mL/½fl oz Cream

Method

Build Black Sambuca and Cointreau then light. Next, pour Baileys and Cream over flaming ingredients.

Garnish: None.

Comments: A novel demonstration of lifestyle cocktails - the heat of the flame illuminates the Black Opal.

Black Russian

Ingredients

Glass: 210mL/7oz Old Fashioned Glass

Mixers: 30mL/1fl oz Vodka

             30mL/1fl oz Kahlúa

Method

Build over ice.

Garnish: Swizzle stick.

Comments: Superb after dinner as Vodka lubricates the way for the scrumptious chocolate Kahlúa.

A dollop of cream on top of the cola in a Hi-Ball glass to stretch the drink.

Tia Maria or Dark Creme de Caco may be substituted for Creme de Cafe, making the drink a **"Black Pearl"**.

Bloody Mary

Ingredients

Glass: 285ml/10oz Hi-Ball Glass

Mixers: 30mL/1fl oz Vodka

           Worchestershire sauce to taste

           120mL/4fl oz Tomato juice

           Tabasco sauce to taste

           Salt and pepper to taste

           Celery salt, optional

Method

Build or shake over ice and strain

Garnish: Stick of celery, slice of lemon.

Comments: Remember to add the spice's first, then Vodka and followed by Tomato juice. Lemon juice and slices are optional ingredients. The celery stick is not part of the garnish, so feel free to nibble as you drink. The glass may also be salt-rimmed. A **"Virgin Mary"** is non alcoholic, with no vodka added. A "Bloody Maria" replaces Vodka with Tequila. Referred to as a **"Stomach Settler"** or **"Livener"**.

Blue Bayou

Ingredients

Glass: 285mL/10oz Hi-Ball Glass

Mixers: 15mL/½fl oz Galliano
15mL/½fl oz Dry Vermouth
30mL/1fl oz Gin
15mL/½fl oz Blue Curacao
top-up with lemonade

Method

Shake with ice and pour.

Garnish: Lemon wheel and mint leaves.

Swizzle stick and straws.

Comments: A prize winning cocktail. Very refreshing cocktail. Perfect for outdoor parties. The yellow of the Galliano can tend to turn the Blue Curacao slightly aqua-green in colour.

Blueberry Delight

Ingredients

Glass: 140mL/5oz Cocktail Glass

Mixers: 30mL/1fl oz Black Sambuca

20mL/²/₃fl oz Coconut Liqueur

10mL/¹/₃fl oz Strawberry Liqueur

60mL/2fl oz Cream

Method

Shake with ice and strain.

Garnish: Strawberry on side of glass with blueberries on a toothpick.

Comments: Find your thrills on these Strawberry and Blueberry hills.

Blue French

Ingredients

Glass: 285mL/10oz Hi-Ball Glass

Mixers: 30mL/1fl oz Pernod
                5mL/¹⁄₆fl ozBlue Curacao Liqueur
                5mL/¹⁄₆fl oz Lemon juice
                top-up with Bitter lemon

Method

Build over ice and stir.

Garnish: Lemon slice on side of glass, swizzle stick and straws.

Comments: A great thirst quencher. Ideal when relaxing by the pool. The publisher's favourite drink.

Blue Hawaii

Ingredients

Glass: 285mL/10oz Hi-Ball Glass

Mixers: 30mL/1fl oz Bacardi
                30mL/1fl oz Blue Curacao Liqueur
                60mL/2fl oz Pineapple juice
                30mL/1fl oz Lemon juice
                30mL/1fl oz Sugar syrup

Method

Build over ice and pour.

Garnish: Pineapple wedge, mint and cherry.
Serve with straws.

Comments: A favourite Hawaiin drink. The mixing of
Pineapple juice and Blue Curacao tends to turn the cocktail
aqua-green in colour.

Bolshoi Punch

Ingredients

Glass: 285ml/9 1/2 oz Footed Hi-Ball Glass

Mixers: 30mL/1fl oz vodka
              10mL/1/3fl oz dark rum
              10mL/1/3fl oz creme de cassis
              15mL/1/2fl oz lime juice
              15mL/1/2fl oz lemon juice
              top up with bitter lemon

Method

Blend with ice and strain then top up with bitter lemon.
Garnish with an orange slice and red cherry.

Bombay Punch

Ingredients

Glass: 285ml/9½ oz Footed Hi-Ball Glass

Mixers: 30mL/1fl oz Cognac
10mL/⅓fl oz dry sherry
10mL/⅓fl oz Cointreau
10mL/⅓fl oz maraschino cherry
20mL/⅔fl oz lemon juice
top up with soda and
Champagne

Method

Blend with ice and strain then top up with soda and
Champagne. Garnish with a red cherry.

Bosom Caresser

Ingredients

Glass: 140mL/5oz Champagne Saucer

Mixers: 30mL/1fl oz Brandy

15mL/½fl oz Orange Liqueur

5mL/⅙fl oz Grenadine Cordial

1 Egg yolk

Method

Shake with ice and strain.

Garnish: Two red cherries, slit on side of glass.

Comments: Close to every lady's heart! Egg yolk allows the cocktail to breathe supporting the Brandy's body and bounce. Fine on any occasion.

Boston Cream

Ingredients

Glass: 120mL/4oz Cocktail Glass, Frosted

Mixers: 30mL/1fl oz cream
15mL/½fl oz triple sec (cointreau)
30mL/1fl oz coconut cream
15mL/½fl oz grenadine

Method

Shake over ice and strain. Garnish with a chocolate cross.

Brandy Alexander

Ingredients

Glass: 140mL/5oz Champagne Saucer

Mixers: 30mL/1fl oz Brandy
30mL/1fl oz Dark Creme de Cacao Liqueur
5mL/⅙fl oz Grenadine Cordial
30mL/1fl oz Cream

Method

Shake with ice and strain.

Garnish: Sprinkle of nutmeg and a cherry.

Comments: An after-dinner cocktail. See 'Helpful Hints' for an easy step-by-step guide on 'How To Make A Brandy Alexander Cross'.

An **"Alexander"** replaces the Cacao with Green Creme de Menthe.

Cognac may be substituted for Brandy to deliver an exceptional after taste.

Cafe Nero

Ingredients

Glass: 140mL/5oz Champagne Saucer

Mixers: 30mL/1fl oz Galliano
Black Coffee
fresh Cream
Sugar

Method

Build, no ice.

Garnish: Grated chocolate.

Comments: Named after Emperor Nero of Rome. Firstly, sprinkle white sugar inside the glass after coating with Galliano. Set Galliano alight and twirl the glass so that flames burn brightly. Pour black coffee gently into glass then layer cream on top of the burning coffee. Sprinkle grated chocolate over the coffee. Also called a **"Roman Coffee"**. Coffee may be served on an accompanying saucer with marshmellows.

Champagne Cocktail

Ingredients

Glass: 140mL/5oz Champagne Flute

Mixers: 1 sugar cube

6 drops of Angostura Bitters

15mL/½fl oz Cognac or brandy

top up with Champagne

Method

Soak sugar cube in Angostura Bitters in flute, before adding brandy, then top with Champagne. Garnish with a red cherry (optional).

Cherries Jubilee

Ingredients

Glass: 140mL/5oz Cocktail Glass

Mixers: 30mL/1fl oz Cherry Advocaat

              30mL/1fl oz White Creme deCacao

              15mL/1/2fl oz Malibu

              40mL/1 1/3fl oz Cream

              15mL/1/2fl oz Milk

Method

Shake with ice and strain.

Garnish: Grated chocolate and cherry and coconut rind on side of glass

Comments: Created by Leah Johns and won first place in Seagram's National Liqueur Championships, Hobart, Tasmania in 1990.

Chiquita

Ingredients

Glass: 285mL/9¹/₂oz Footed Hi-Ball Glass

Mixers: 45mL/1¹/₂fl oz vodka

10mL/¹/₃fl oz banana liqueur

10mL/¹/₃fl oz lime juice

half a sliced banana

pinch of sugar

Method

Blend with ice and pour. Garnish with banana slices.
Top with bitter lemon.

Chivas Manhattan

Ingredients

Glass: 90mL/3oz Cocktail Glass

Mixers: 1 shot Chivas Regal Scotch Whiskey
$^1/_2$ shot Dry Vermouth
$^1/_2$ shot Sweet Vermouth
Dash of Grand Mariner
Burnt Orange Zest

Method

Place ice cubes in glass, pour in Chivas Regal, Dry & Sweet Vermouth and a dash of Grand Marnier. Stir thoroughly and strain into another chilled glass. Slice a piece of orange peel, set fire to the squeezed zest and place in the glass and enjoy.

Garnish: None

Comments: An interesting change to a "traditional" Manhattan cocktail.

Chivas Royal

Ingredients

Glass: Champagne Flute

Mixers: 1 shot Chivas Regal Scotch Whiskey
1 dash Apple Schnapps
Ginger Ale

Method

Half fill a chilled champagne flute with crushed ice. Pour in Chivas Regal, add Apple Schnapps (or clear apple juice if preferred). Top up with Ginger Ale.

Garnish: Place a slice of green apple into the drink and serve.

Comments: A drink fit for a King.

Cointreau Caipirinha

Ingredients

Glass: 175mL/6oz Prism Rocks Glass

Mixers: 30mL/1fl oz Cointreau

¹/₄ fresh lime or lemon

crushed ice

Method

Cut lime into pieces and place in glass. Extract juice by using the Cointreau Pestle, fill glass with crushed ice and add Cointreau and mini pestle. Stir.

The pestle is a new Cointreau product which assists in the initial extraction of the lime or lemon juice.

Daiquiri

Ingredients

Glass: 140mL/5oz Champagne Saucer

Mixers: 45mL/1½fl oz Rum

            30mL/1fl oz Pure Lemon Juice

            15mL/½fl oz Sugar syrup

            ½ egg white, optional

Method

Shake with ice and strain.

Garnish: Lemon slice or lemon spiral.

Comments: Most Australian cocktail bars do not use egg white, however it definitely enhances the Daiquiri's appearance. Ideal for large parties as batches can be stored ready for instant use. Mango, when in season, is very popular. When mixing a pure fruit daiquiri, it is best to use an electric blender and blend well with ice, then strain into a champagne saucer.

Death In The Afternoon

Ingredients

Glass: 140mL/5oz Champagne Flute

Mixers: 15mL/½fl oz Pernod

Champagne

Method

Build, no Ice.

Garnish: None.

Comments: Ernest Hemingway's favourite cocktail.
A bubbly occasion deserves this fully imported French
aphrodisiac mixer.

Depth Charge

Ingredients

Glass: 425mL/14oz Schooner Beer Glass

20mL/²/₃fl oz Liqueur Glass

Mixers: 400mL/13oz Beer

20mL/²/₃fl oz Drambuie*

Method

Build, no ice

Garnish: None

Comments: Fill schooner, pot or beer mug with beer 3-5 centimetres below the glass rim. Toast by touching liqueur glasses filled with Drambuie before sliding into the beer glass. You'll be amazed that the Drambuie remains in the liqueur glass due to its higher density.

*Drambuie may be substituted with Lochan Ora

Dizzy Blonde

Ingredients

Glass: 285mL/9½oz Hi-Ball Glass

Mixers: 60mL/2fl oz Advocaat

              30mL/1fl oz Pernod

              top up with lemonade

Method

Shake over ice and pour then top up with lemonade.
Garnish with an orange slice and cherry.

Double Jeopardy

Ingredients

Glass: 285mL/10oz Hi-Ball Glass

Mixers: 45mL/1½fl oz Frangelico
45mL/1½fl oz Black Sambuca
scoop of Vanilla ice cream
top-up with Milk

Method

Blend with Ice and Stir.

Garnish: Scooper spoon (long teaspoon) and straws.

Comments: Take a chance on this cocktail. Remember you can't be tried for the same crime twice. Great in winter by the open fire.

Dubonnet Cocktail

Ingredients

Glass: 120mL/4oz Cocktail Glass, chilled

Mixers: 30mL/1fl oz Dubonnet

15mL/½fl oz gin

1 dash orange bitters

Method

Build over ice. Garnish with a lemon twist.

El Burro

Ingredients

Glass: 285mL/10oz Fancy Cocktail Glass

Mixers: 15mL/½fl oz Kahlúa
15mL/½fl oz Rum
30mL/1fl oz Coconut cream
30mL/1fl oz Cream
½ Banana

Method

Blend with ice and strain.

Garnish: Banana and mint leaves.

Comments: A full and thick style of cocktail, very popular at the moment. Definitely and afternoon cocktail.

Evergreen

Ingredients

Glass: 90mL/3oz Cocktail Glass

Mixers: 15mL/½fl oz Dry Vermouth
                 30mL/1fl oz Dry Gin
                 15mL/½fl oz Melon Liqueur
                 7mL/⅙fl oz Blue Curacao Liqueur

Method

Stir over ice and strain.

Garnish: Red cherry on lip of glass

Comments: Stir the first three ingredients of this pre-dinner cocktail over ice and strain into cocktail glass. Then drop the Blue Curacao creating a visible layer. A poignant tasting cocktail consumed in summer.

Fallen Angel (Australian Version)

Ingredients

Glass: 285mL/10oz Hi-Ball Glass

Mixers: 20mL/²/₃fl oz Advocaat Liqueur
20mL/²/₃fl oz Cherry Brandy
top-up with lemonade

Method

Build over ice and stir.

Garnish: Red cherry or strawberry. Serve with straws.

Comments: Although requiring individual taste bud approval, ensure Advocaat and Cherry Brandy is mixed thoroughly before topping up with Lemonade.

A **"Ruptured Rooster"** doesn't require the ingredients to be mixed.

Fluffy Duck (No. 1)

Ingredients

Glass: 285mL/10oz Hi-Ball Glass

Mixers: 30mL/1fl oz Rum

30mL/1fl oz Advocaat Liqueur

top-up with lemonade

cream, floated

Method

Build over ice.

Garnish: Orange slice and a red cherry. Serve with straws.

Comments: Most cocktail bars shake ingredients with cream before topping up with lemonade. When using a post mix gun, squirt the lemonade directly into the middle of the liquid surface instead of spraying against the back of the glass. This gives a billowing cloud effect.

Fluffy Duck (No. 2)

Ingredients

Glass:　　140mL/5oz Champagne Saucer

Mixers:　　30mL/1fl oz Rum

　　　　　　30mL/1fl oz Advocaat

　　　　　　30mL/1fl oz Orange juice

　　　　　　30mL/1fl oz Cream

Method

Shake with ice and strain.

Garnish: Orange slice and a red cherry.

Comments: An after-dinner variation of the popular Fluffy Duck cocktail. A smoother and shorter drink.

Frappe

Ingredients

Glass: 90mL/3oz Cocktail Glass

Mixers: 30mL/1fl oz of preferred liqueur
                 (e.g. Green Crème de Menthe Liqueur)

Method

Build over crushed ice.

Garnish: Two short straws

Comments: Spoon the required quantity of crushed ice into the glass. Create spectacular rainbow effects with small quantities of liqueurs. Green Crème de Menthe is highly recommended because it acts as a breath freshener after dessert.

Freddy-Fud-Pucker

Ingredients

Glass: 285mL/10oz Hi-Ball Glass

Mixers: 30mL/1fl oz Tequila

120mL/4fl oz Orange juice

15mL/¹/₂fl oz Galliano, floated

Method

Build over ice.

Garnish: Orange slice and red cherry.
Serve with straws.

Comments: Fantastic when drinking with friends – each participant after drinking half the cocktail says very quickly, 3 times. "Freddy Fud Puckers Fud any Puck". The first to be caught out is obliged to buy the next round. Be sure to mind your 'p's and 'f's when ordering.

French Fantasy

Ingredients

Glass: 140mL/5oz Cocktail Glass

Mixers: 30mL/1fl oz Creme de Grand Marnier

30mL/1fl oz Vodka

15mL/½fl oz Tia Maria

30mL/1fl oz Pineapple juice

30mL/1fl oz Orange juice

Method

Shake with ice and strain.

Garnish: Banana slice and red cherry.

Comments: Creme de Grand Marnier is similar to Bailey's. This cocktail is really smooth and easy to drink.

Geisha

Ingredients

Glass: 135mL/4½ oz Tulip Champagne Glass

Mixers: 30mL/1fl oz Bourbon

30mL/1fl oz sake

10mL/⅓fl oz lemon juice

10mL/⅓fl oz sugar syrup

Method

Shake over ice and strain. Garnish with a red cherry

Georgia Peach

Ingredients

Glass: 285mL/9½ oz Hi-Ball Glass

Mixers: 30mL/1fl oz Bacardi

               30mL/1fl oz Peach Liqueur

               90mL/3fl oz cranberry juice

Method

Build over ice and pour. Garnish with a peach slice.

Gibson

Ingredients

Glass: 120mL/4oz Cocktail Glass

Mixers: 60mL/2fl oz gin

10mL/¹⁄₃fl oz dry vermouth

Method

Shake over ice and strain. Garnish with one cocktail onion.

Gimlet

Ingredients

Glass: 175mL/6oz Prism Rocks Glass

Mixers: 60mL/2fl oz gin

30mL/1fl oz lime juice

Method

Shake over ice and pour then add cubed ice. Garnish with two cocktail onions on toothpicks sunk in glass.

God Daughter

Ingredients

Glass: 140mL/5oz Champagne Saucer

Mixers: 30mL/1fl oz Sambuca

              30mL/1fl oz Amaretto di Saronno

              30mL/1fl ozcream

              5mL/⅙fl oz Grenadine Cordial

Method

Shake with ice and strain.

Garnish: Chocolate flake, strawberry and mint.

Comments: Ideal cocktail after Italian food.

God Father

Ingredients

Glass: 185mL/6oz Old Fashioned Spirit Glass

Mixers: 30mL/1fl oz Scotch Whisky

30mL/1fl oz Amaretto di Saronno

Method

Build over ice.

Garnish: None

Comments: To be drunk as either a pre-dinner drink or a night-cap. The guiding hand of Amaretto tempers the boldness of the Scotch.

Golden Cadillac

Ingredients

Glass: 140mL/5oz Cocktail Glass

Mixers: 30mL/1fl oz Galliano

30mL/1fl oz White Crème de Cacao
Liqueur

30mL/1fl oz Cream

Method

Shake with ice and strain.

Garnish: Red cherry or strawberry

Comments: The distilled Cocoa Beans will take you for the ride of your life. Cruise through this cocktail in luxurious style. Essential for all cocktail parties. Anywhere, anytime.

Golden Dream

Ingredients

Glass: 140mL/5oz Cocktail Glass

Mixers: 30mL/²⁄₃fl oz Galliano
20mL/²⁄₃fl oz Cointreau*
20mL/²⁄₃fl oz Orange Juice
20mL/²⁄₃fl oz Cream

Method

Shake with ice and strain.

Garnish: Red cherry on a toothpick on side of glass.

Comments: Chilled Orange Juice tarts the Galliano and freezes the Cointreau leaving a creamy tangy lining from your throat to your toes. Cointreau may be replaced with Triple Sec.

Gomango

Ingredients

Glass: 440mL/14oz Hurricane Glass

Mixers: 15mL/½fl oz Triple Sec Liqueur

15mL/½fl oz White Crème de Cacao

15mL/½fl oz Cherry Advocaat Liqueur

15mL/½fl oz Orange juice

15mL/½fl oz Cream

1 cheek of fresh Mango

Method

Blend with ice.

Garnish: Butterfly strawberry on side of glass.

Comments: Created by Con Pandelakia, winner of 1991 Australian Title.

Grasshopper

Ingredients

Glass: 140mL/5oz champagne Saucer

Mixers: 30mL/1fl oz Crème de Menthe Liqueur

30mL/1fl oz White Crème de Cacao

30mL/1fl oz Cream

Method

Shake with ice and strain.

Garnish: 2 red cherries slit on the side of the glass.

Comments: Jump right into this very popular after dinner cocktails. Some people prefer Dark Crème de Cacao instead of White Crème de Cacao. Shake until smooth

G.R.B.

Ingredients

Glass: 90mL/3oz Cocktail Glass

Mixers: 30mL/1fl oz Galliano
10mL/$^1/_3$fl oz Grenadine Cordial
30mL/1fl oz Rum

Method

Build over ice.

Garnish: Float 1 mint leaf.

Comments: Anyone who stalls gets a double-hit-round. The mint permeates the Rum leaving a refreshingly sweet aftertaste. Please use your imagination to name this acronym!

Greek God

Ingredients

Glass: Whisky Shot

Mixers: 15mL/½fl oz ouzo
               15mL/½fl oz Pernod

Method

Pour in order then shoot.

Green with Envy

Ingredients

Glass: 210mL/7oz Hurricane Glass

Mixers: 30mL/1fl oz Ouzo

            30mL/1fl oz Blue Curacao Liqueur

            120mL/4fl oz Pineapple juice

Method

Shake with ice and pour.

Garnish: Pineapple spear with leaves and cherry. Serve with straws.

Comments: An afternoon cocktail. The aniseed in Oyzo chills the pungent Pineapple Juice. As they say... Jealousy's a curse, Envy is worse.

Harvey Wallbanger

Ingredients

Glass: 285mL/9oz Hi-Ball Glass

Mixers: 40mL/1¹/₃fl oz Vodka

               125mL/4fl oz Orange juice

               15mL/¹/₂fl oz Galliano, floated

Method

Build over ice.

Garnish: Orange slice and cherry.
Swizzle stick and straws.

Comments: The local Hawaiian bartenders will tell you a visiting Irishman called Harvey pin-balled down the corridor to hotel room after a night out. Hence, he was known a "Harvey Wallbanger".

Hawaiian Punch

Ingredients

Glass: 285mL/9½oz Hi-Ball Glass

Mixers: 20mL/⅔fl oz Southern Comfort
20mL/⅔fl oz amaretto
15mL/½fl oz vodka
40mL/1⅓fl oz pineapple juice
40mL/1⅓fl oz orange juice
20mL/⅔fl oz lime juice
20mL/⅔fl oz grenadine

Method

Shake over ice and pour then add grenadine. Garnish with orange slice and a red cherry.

Hurricane

Ingredients

Glass: 210mL/7oz Hurricane Glass

Mixers: 30mL/1fl oz Bacardi
30mL/1fl oz orange juice
15mL/½fl oz lime cordial
45mL/1½fl oz lemon juice
45mL/1½fl oz sugar syrup
top with 15mL/½fl oz Bacardi Gold

Method

Shake with ice and pour.
Garnish with orange slice and cherry. Serve with straws.

Irish Coffee

Ingredients

Glass: 250mL/8oz Irish Coffee Glass

Mixers: 30mL/1fl oz Baileys Irish Cream
1 teaspoon brown sugar
top-up with hot black coffee
float fresh Cream

Method
Build (no ice).

Garnish: Chocolate flake optional.

Comments: The most widely drunk liqueur coffe which verifies its approval amongst coffee lovers. Tullamore Dew & Jameson's are most popular Irish Whiskies. Other liqueur coffees are: **French – Brandy, English – Gin, Russian – Vodka, American – Bourbon, Calypso – Dark Rum, Jamaican – Tia Maria, Parisienne – Grand Marnier, Mexican – Kahlúa, Monks – Benedictine, Scottish – Scotch, Canadian – Rye.**

Japanese Slipper

Ingredients

Glass: 90mL/3oz Cocktail Glass

Mixers: 30mL/1fl oz Melon Liqueur
30mL/1fl oz Cointreau
30mL/1fl oz Lemon juice

Method

Shake with ice and strain

Garnish: Slice of lemon on side of glass.

Comments: Simple to prepare and the habit preferences of consumers has ensured this cocktail will remain one most often requested. Pouring 5ml Grenadine upon completion of the cocktail gives a marvellous visual effect and sweetens the sour element.

Jelly Bean

Ingredients

Glass: 285mL/9oz Hi-ball glass

Mixers: 30mL/1fl oz Ouzo

15mL/½fl oz Blue Curacao Liqueur

15mL/½fl oz Grenadine Cordial

Top-up with Lemonade

Method

Build over ice.

Garnish: Swizzle stick and straws. Red cherry dropped into glass.

Comments: A cool liquid confectionery. Dropping Blue Curacao and Grenadine into the cocktail after presenting to the customer gives a swirling lollipop effect. Regularly drunk without the Blue Curacao.

Kamikaze

Ingredients

Glass: 140mL/5oz Cocktail Glass

Mixers: 30mL/1fl oz Vodka

30mL/1fl oz Cointreau

30mL/1fl oz fresh lemon juice

5mL/½fl oz Lime cordial

Method

Shake with ice and strain.

Garnish: Red cocktail onion on a toothpick in the glass.

Comments: Maintain freshness for larger volumes by adding stained egg white. Mix in a jug and keep refrigerated. For the hyper-active. Cointreau may be replaced with Triple Sec.

Kelly's Comfort

Ingredients

Glass: 285mL/9½ oz Hi-Ball Glass

Mixers: 30mL/1fl oz Southern Comfort
30mL/1fl oz Baileys Irish Cream
30mL/1fl oz milk
4 strawberries
15mL/½fl oz sugar syrup

Method

Blend over ice and pour. Garnish with a strawberry.

K.G.B.

Ingredients

Glass: 185mL/6oz Old Fashioned Spirit Glass

Mixers: 30mL/1fl oz Kahlúa

               30mL/1fl oz Grand Marnier

               30mL/1fl oz Baileys Irish Cream

Method

Build over ice.

Garnish: None

Comments: The first letter of each of the ingredients give this cocktail its name. A late night party drink.

Kick in the Balls

Ingredients

Glass: 140mL/5oz Champagne Saucer

Mixers: 30mL/1fl oz Rum

             30mL/1fl oz Orange Juice

             30mL/1fl oz Melon Liqueur

             30mL/1fl oz Cream

             15mL/$\frac{1}{2}$fl oz Coconut Cream

Method

Shake with ice and strain.

Garnish: Two melon balls previously marinated in the Coruba Rum.

Comments: Float melon balls. Using a toothpick, eat both balls together and you'll be sure to feel a "Kick in the Balls". Refridgerate melon balls to preserve their freshness.

Kir

Ingredients

Glass: 140mL/5oz Wine Goblet

Mixers: 15mL/½fl oz Cassis Liqueur
                     Top-up with dry White Wine

Method

Build, no ice.

Garnish: None.

Comments: A superb pre-dinner drink. Use cold dry wines. Do not spoil the drink by using more than 15mL/½fl oz of Cassis Liqueur. To make a "Kir Imperial" substitute 5mL/⅙fl oz Grenadine for 15mL/½fl oz Cassis. "Kir Royale" is served in a 140mL/5oz champagne flute with a good dash of Cassis liqueur and toped with the best champagne available.

Hint: Sprinkle a thumb pinch of sugar to produce fizzy bubbles from the champagne. Served chilled.

Lady M

Ingredients

Glass: 285mL/9oz Hurricane Glass

Mixers: 45mL/1½fl oz Frangelico

45mL/1½fl oz Melon Liqueur

2 scoops vanilla ice cream

Garnish: Strawberry on side of glass sprinkled with grated chocolate.

Comments: Blend for more than 20 seconds to thoroughly mix ingredients. Be adventurous and try various flavoured ice-creams.

Lamborghini

Ingredients

Glass: 90mL/3oz Cocktail Glass

Mixers: 20mL/²/₃fl oz Crème de Café Liqueur

20mL/²/₃fl oz Cointreau

20mL/²/₃fl oz Sambuca

Cold Fresh Cream

Method

Build, no ice.

Garnish: Grated chocolate flakes.

Comments: Layer ingredients in the above order using a spoon, then float fresh cream. As the name suggests, speed is the object of this cocktail. You may like to try drinking each layered ingredient through a straw at a quickening speed; similar to changing the gears in a Lamborgini.

Lamborghini (Flaming)

Ingredients

Glass: 4-6 Tall Dutch Cordial Glasses

Mixers: 22mL/²/₃fl oz Kahlua
22mL/²/₃fl oz Cointreau per cocktail
22mL/²/₃fl oz Sambuca
Cold Fresh cream

Method

Heat and build.

Garnish: Grated chocolate flake.

Comments: Warm alcoholic ingredients in a stainless steel saucepan. Be sure to simmer flame to avoid scorching Kahlua. Stand glasses in a row and allow flame to burn for 10-15 seconds. Pour cold cream into a spoon and float onto the cocktail to extinguish flame. The nightclub version replaces Sambuca for Green Chartreuse as it is distinct in colour, easier to layer and also flamed.

Leprechaun

Ingredients

Glass: 210mL Old Fashioned Glass

Mixers: 60mL/2fl oz Irish Whiskey
top up with tonic water

Method

Build over ice. Garnish with a lime slice dropped into the glass.

Lights of Havana

Ingredients

Glass: 285mL/9½ oz Hi-Ball Glass

Mixers: 60mL/2fl oz soda water
45mL/1½fl oz Malibu
30mL/1fl oz Midori
60mL/2fl oz orange juice
60mL/2fl oz pineapple juice

Method

Shake over ice and pour. Garnish with a straw and a lime wheel.

Lip Sip Suck

Ingredients

Glass: Whiskey Shot

Mixers: 30mL/1fl oz tequila
lemon in quarters or slices
salt

Method

Pour tequila into glass. On the flat piece of skin between the base of your thumb and index finger, place a pinch of salt. Place a quarter of the lemon by you on the bar. Lick the salt off your hand, shoot the tequila and then suck the lemon in quick succession.

Long Island Iced Tea

Ingredients

Glass: 285mL/9oz Hi-Ball Glass

Mixers: 30mL/1fl ozVodka
30mL/1fl oz Lemon juice
30mL/1fl oz Tequila
30mL/1fl oz Sugar syrup
30mL/1fl oz White Rum
dash of Cola
30mL/1fl oz Cointreau

Method

Build over Ice.

Garnish: Lemon twist and mint leaves. Serve with straws.

Comments: The tea coloured cola is splashed into the cocktail making it slightly unsuitable for a "Tea Party". Many variations are concocted using different white spirits. American by design, Australians know it better as a **"Long Island Iced Tea".** It is strongly recommended that you consume no more than one.

Louisiana Lullaby

Ingredients

Glass: 90mL/3oz Cocktail Glass

Mixers: 30mL/1fl oz dark rum
              10mL/¹/₃fl oz Dubonnet
              5mL/¹/₆fl oz Grand Marnier

Method

Shake over ice and strain. Garnish with a twist of lemon.

Madame Butterfly

Ingredients

Glass: 140mL/5oz Margarita Glass

Mixers: 1. 30mL/1fl oz Passoa
15mL/½fl oz Melon Liqueur
15mL/½fl oz White Creme de Cacao
30mL/1fl oz Pineapple Juice
2. 30mL/1fl oz Cream
15mL/½fl oz Melon Liqueur

Method

1. Shake with ice and strain.
2. Layered Melon Liqueur and Cream.

Garnish: Strawberry and Butterfly.

Comments: *This cocktail requires two shakers. In one hand, shake the first four ingredients over ice and strain. In the other hand, shake Melon Liqueur and Cream, then layer. An innovative award winning cocktail.*

Mai-Tai

Ingredients

Glass: 285mL/9oz Hi-Ball Glass

Mixers: 30mL/1fl oz Rum
                 30mL/1fl oz Lemon juice
                 15mL/$\frac{1}{2}$fl oz Amaretto di Saronno
                 30mL/1fl oz Sugar syrup
                 15mL/$\frac{1}{2}$fl oz Rum
                 $\frac{1}{2}$ fresh Lime juiced
                 30mL/1fl oz Orange Curacao Liqueur

Method

Shake with ice and pour.

Garnish: Pineapple spear, mint leaves, tropical flowers if possible (e.g. Singapore Orchid), lime shell. Serve with straws.

Comments: A well known rum-based refreshing tropical cocktail. Grenadine is often added to redden a glowing effect while the Rum may be floated on top when served without straws. Rum lovers drink their Mai Tais this way. It can also be built into a tall glass and stirred with the pineapple spear.

Malibu Magic

Ingredients

Glass: 285mL/9oz Hurricane Glass

Mixers: 30mL/1fl oz Malibu*
30mL/1fl oz Strawberry Liqueur
30mL/1fl oz Orange juice
3-4 fresh strawberries
60mL/2fl oz Cream

Method

Blend with ice and pour.

Garnish: A single strawberry and twisted orange peel.

Comments: Shake to the wonders of Californian dreaming.
*Malibu may be substituted with Coconut Liqueur. 15mL/½
fl oz of Cointreau may be added for that magic moment.

Manhattan

Ingredients

Glass: 150mL/5oz Cocktail Glass

Mixers: 30mL/1fl oz Bourbon

                15mL/½fl oz rosso vermouth

                dash Angostura Bitters

Method

Stir over ice and strain. Garnish with a red cherry on toothpick in glass.

A pre dinner cocktail. Replace Rosso Vermouth with Cinzano Dry, add a twist of lemon and you have instantly mixed a Dry Manhattan.

Rye whisky may be substituted for Bourbon.

Margarita

Ingredients

Glass: 140mL/5oz Margarita Glass, salt-rimmed

Mixers: 30mL/1fl oz Tequila

              30mL/1fl oz Lemon Juice

              15mL/½fl oz Cointreau

              ½ egg white, optional

Method

Shake with Ice and Strain.

Garnish: Lemon wheel on edge of glass.

Comments: Margarita's can be 'shaken' or 'frozen' – a professional bartender will always ask which method is preferred. A "Frozen Margarita" (Sorbet) contains $1/3$ of the blender full of ice. Add water if the mix becomes gluggy.

Martini

Ingredients

Glass: 90mL/3oz Cocktail Glass

Mixers: 45mL/1½fl oz Gin

20mL/⅔fl oz Dry Vermouth

Method

Stir over ice and strain.

Garnish: Lemon twist or olive on toothpick in the glass.

Comments: The classically sophisticated black-tie cocktail. Always stirred, however, when shaken it is known as a **"Bradford"**. An olive garnish retains the Gin sting wheres a lemon twist makes the cocktail smoother.

Note: A "Dry Martini" has less Vermouth.

Midori Avalanche

Ingredients

Glass: 285mL/9oz Hurricane Glass

Mixers: 30mL/1fl oz Blue Curacao

           30mL/1fl oz Melon Liqueur

           15mL/1/2fl oz Triple Sec Liqueur

           60mL/2fl oz Pineapple Juice

Method

Pour Blue Curacao into glass. Blend other ingredients with ice and pour.

Garnish: Triangle of pineapple on side of glass.

Comments: This deep sea cocktail can be found at pool bars around Australia. Be sure to use plenty of ice to quench a hot dry thirst.

Mint Julep

Ingredients

Glass: 285mL/9½ oz Tom Collins Glass

Mixers: 60mL/2fl oz Bourbon

1 teaspoon sugar

2-3 dashes cold water or club soda

8 sprigs of fresh mint

crushed or shaved ice

Method

Muddle sugar, water and 5 mint sprigs in a glass. Pour into thoroughly frosted glass and pack with ice. Add bourbon and mix (with a chopping motion using a long-handled bar spoon). Garnish with remaining mint and serve with a straw. Tear mint leaves slightly before sugaring for greater aroma.

Monkey Gland

Ingredients

Glass: 120mL/4oz Cocktail Glass

Mixers: 30mL/1fl oz gin

10mL/⅓fl oz apple juice

5mL/⅙fl oz parfait amour

5mL/⅙fl oz grenadine

Method

Shake with ice and strain

Garnish with an orange twist.

Variation: substitute 20mL/⅔fl oz Pernod for the Parfait Amour and Grenadine.

Montmartre

Ingredients

Glass: 90mL/3oz Cocktail Glass

Mixers: 10mL/⅓fl oz Cointreau

30mL/1fl oz gin

10mL/⅓fl oz sweet vermouth

Method

Coat glass with Cointreau then pour Gilbey's Gin and Cinzano Sweet Vermouth over ice. Garnish with a red cherry. From the world renowned painters courtyard next to Sacré Coeur that overlooks Paris.

Moscow Mule

Ingredients

Glass: 285mL/9oz Hi-Ball Glass

Mixers: 30mL/1fl oz Vodka

15mL/1⁄2fl oz lime cordial

top-up with ginger beer

Method

Build over ice.

Garnish: Slice of lemon and mint. Straws and swizzle stick.

Comments: A long, cool, refreshing cocktail. It tastes a lot better if the juice of half a lime is squeezed into the cocktail in place of the lime cordial.

Mount Temple

Ingredients

Glass: 90mL/3oz Cocktail Glass

Mixers: 30mL/1fl oz Kahlúa
30mL/1fl oz Tequila
30mL/1fl oz Coconut Liqueur

Method

Build over ice.

Garnish: Dollop of cream in centre of glass.

Comments: Love is a temple and you'll love this higher ground.

Negroni

Ingredients

Glass: 90mL/3oz Cocktail Glass

Mixers: 20mL/²/₃fl oz Campari

20mL/²/₃fl oz sweet vermouth

10mL/¹/₃fl oz gin

Method

Shake with ice and strain. Garnish with a twist of lemon
and orange peel.

Old Fashioned – Scotch

Ingredients

Glass: 285mL/9oz Old Fashioned Spirit Glass

Mixers: 30mL/1fl oz Scotch Whisky
                       Angostura Bitters
                       sugar cube
                       soda water

Method

Build over ice.

Garnish: ½ slice of orange and lemon and a cherry.
A swizzle stick may be used.

Comments: Splash Bitters evenly over the sugar cube before adding ice, Scotch and topping up with soda. A soothing 'knocking-off' drink after 5 pm. Ensure cherries are dry. If cherries are moist, the juice may taint the flavour, thereby marring the appearance of the Scotch. Bourbon and Rye Whisky may be served in the "**Old Fashioned**" way.

Ole

Ingredients

Glass: 90mL/3oz Cocktail Glass

Mixers: 30mL/1fl oz Tequila
30mL/1fl oz Banana Liqueur
10mL/⅓fl oz Blue Curacao Liqueur

Method

Stir over ice and strain.

Garnish: Lemon wheel

Comments: 1988 World Cocktail Championship winner.
Stir the Tequila and Banana Liqueur gently over ice to
avoid 'bruising' and strain into the glass, then drop Blue
Curacao. It not only looks good but is great to drink.
Easy to make if you're in a hurry.

Orgasm

Ingredients

Glass: 210mL/7oz Old Fashioned Spirit Glass

Mixers: 22mL/²⁄₃fl oz Baileys Irish Cream
                22mL/²⁄₃fl oz Cointreau

Method

Build over ice.

Garnish: Strawberry or cherries, optional

Comments: Probably the most widely drunk cocktail in Australia and very popular with the ladies.

A "**Multiple Orgasm**" is made with the addition of 30ml of fresh Cream or Milk.

A "**Screaming Multiple Orgasm**" has the addition of 15ml Galliano along with 30ml fresh Cream or Milk.

Pago Pago

Ingredients

Glass: 250mL/8oz Old Fashioned

Mixers: 30mL/1fl oz Bacardi Gold Rum
10mL/¹/₃fl oz lime juice
10mL/¹/₃fl oz pineapple juice
5mL/¹/₆fl oz green Chartreuse
5mL/¹/₆fl oz Cointreau

Method

Shake with ice and strain over 3 cube of ice. Garnish with a
pineapple wedge and a cherry.

Palm Sundae

Ingredients

Glass: 285mL/9oz Hurricane Glass

Mixers: 45mL/1½fl oz Peach Liqueur
30mL/1fl oz Coconut Liqueur
15mL/½fl oz Banana Liqueur
60mL/2fl oz Tropical Fruit Juice
3 fresh strawberries

Method

Blend with ice and pour.

Garnish: Orange wedge, pineapple leaves and Maraschino cherry.

Comments: *Peach liqueur is dynamically exquisite in this specially designed cocktail recipe. The succulent peach flavour is another member in the new generation of natural tropical fruit cocktails.*

Picasso

Ingredients

Glass: 90mL/3oz Cocktail Glass

Mixers: 30mL/1fl oz Cognac
               10mL/¹/₃fl oz Dubonnet
               10mL/¹/₃fl oz lime juice
               15mL/¹/₂fl oz sugar syrup

Method

Shake over ice and strain. Garnish with an orange twist.

Pimm's No. 1 Cup

Ingredients

Glass: 285mL/9oz Hi-Ball Glass

Mixers: 30-45ml Pimm's No. 1 Cup
                top-up with either lemonade or dry ginger
                or equal parts of both

Method

Build over ice.

Garnish: Orange and lemon slice, cherries, cucumber skin, swizzle stick and straws.

Comments: A slice of orange can detract from the sweet aftertaste. Slicing the inside of the cucumber skin allows the small drops to keep the drink chilled. Originally 6 Pimm's numbers were commonly consumed, today there are only two. Pimm's No.1 – Gin base, Pimm's No. 2 – Vodka base. Often referred to as the **"Fruit Cocktail Cocktail"**.

Pina Colada

Ingredients

Glass: 285ml/9oz Hi-ball Glass

Mixers: 30mL/1fl oz Rum
30mL/1fl oz Coconut Cream
30mL/1fl oz Sugar Syrup
125mL/4fl oz Unsweetened Pineapple juice

Method

Shake with ice and pour.

Garnish: Pineapple wedge - three leaves and a cherry.
Straws & swizzle stick.

Comments: Another tropical Hawaiian cocktail which is
distinguished by including Coconut Cream. Unfortunately,
it is not normally stocked by Australian bars. If temporarily
unavailable, Coconut Liqueur will suffice. Cream is optional
for a richer blend.

Pink Panther

Ingredients

Glass: 140mL/5oz Champagne Saucer

Mixers: 22mL/²/₃fl oz Bourbon
30mL/1fl oz Vodka
15mL/1½fl oz Malibu
40mL/1¹/₃fl oz Cream
dash Grenadine

Method

Shake with ice and strain

Garnish: Cherry and mint.

Comments: Leap out of a 'pink fit' with one of the first cocnut cocktails made in Australia. For the intrepid.

Planters Punch

Ingredients

Glass: 150mL/5oz Cocktail Glass

Mixers: 30mL/1fl oz dark rum

30mL/1fl oz lemon or lime juice

60mL/2fl oz orange juice

5mL/⅙fl oz grenadine

Method

Build over ice then add dash of grenadine. Garnish with fruit slices.

Polish Sidecar

Ingredients

Glass: 90mL/3oz Cocktail Glass

Mixers: 20mL/²⁄₃fl oz gin

                 20mL/²⁄₃fl oz lemon juice

                 10mL/¹⁄₃fl oz raspberry liqueur

Method

Shake with gin and lemon juice with ice and pour then float raspberry liqueur. Garnish with raspberries.

Polynesia

Ingredients

Glass: 135mL/4½oz Tulip Champagne Glass

Mixers: 30mL/1fl oz white rum

               30mL/1fl oz melon liqueur

               10mL/⅓fl oz lime juice

               half egg white

Method

Blend with ice and pour. Garnish with banana.

Prairie Oyster

Ingredients

Glass: 90mL/3oz Cocktail Glass

Mixers: 30mL/1fl oz Brandy

Salt and pepper

Worcestershire Sauce

Tabasco Sauce

1 Egg yolk

Method

Build, no ice.

Garnish: None

Comments: the spices relieve a sore head and the Brandy replenishes lost energy. Brandy may be replaced with any spirit of your choice, however cold Vodka is medically soothing. Best before breakfast.

Pretty Woman

Ingredients

Glass: 285mL/9oz Hurricane Glass

Mixers: **Blender 1**
30mL/1fl oz Melon Liqueur
30mL/1fl oz Malibu
Blender 2
30mL/1fl oz Strawberry Liqueur
3-4 strawberries

Method

Blend with ice in two separate blenders and pour.
Garnish: Strawberry and umbrella on side of glass.

Comments: Remember to tilt the glass when pouring the two sets of ingredients into the glass. Choosing a long glass will assist you. Very alcoholic as there is no juice. A kaleidoscope of colour for you to enjoy.

P.S. I Love You

Ingredients

Glass: 150mL/5oz Champagne Saucer

Mixers: 30mL/1fl oz Amaretto

30mL/1fl oz Kahlúa

30mL/1fl oz Baileys Irish Cream

5mL/^{1}/$_6$fl oz grenadine

Method

Build over ice and stir. Garnish with sprinkled nutmeg.

Quebec

Ingredients

Glass: 120mL/4oz Cocktail Glass

Mixers: 30mL/1fl oz Canadian Club Whisky

10mL/⅓fl oz dry Vermouth

10mL/⅓fl oz Amer Picon

10mL/⅓fl oz maraschino liqueur

Method

Shake over ice and strain. Garnish with a cocktail onion. Amer Picon is a French brand of bitters that derives much of its flavour from gentian root and oranges. 2 dashes Angostura Bitters may be substituted.

Raffles Singapore Sling

Ingredients

Glass: 285mL/9oz Hi-Ball Glass

Mixers: 30mL/1fl oz Gin
              30mL/1fl oz Orange juice
              30mL/1fl oz Cherry Brandy Liqueur
              30mL/1fl oz lime juice
              15mL/½fl oz Triple Sec Liqueur
              30mL/1fl oz Pineapple juice
              dash Angostura Bitters
              15mL/½fl oz Benedictine

Method

Shake with ice and pour.

Garnish: Orange slice, mint, a cherry, swizzle stick and straws.

Comments: This recipe is the original Singapore version, with its fruit juices it tastes totally different from some Gin Slings commonly served in bars.

Red Eye

Ingredients

Glass: 140mL Cocktail Glass

Mixers: 210mL/7fl oz beer

90mL/3fl oz tomato juice

Method

Build no ice.

Rocket Fuel

Ingredients

Glass: 210mL/7oz Old Fashioned Spirit Glass

Mixers: 15mL/¹⁄₂fl oz Rum

15mL/¹⁄₂fl oz Dry Gin

15mL/¹⁄₂fl oz Vodka

30mL/1fl oz Lemonade

15mL/¹⁄₂fl oz Tequila

Method

Build over ice.

Garnish: Swizzle stick.

Comments: This cocktail secured it's bar fame when Australia's rock legend Jimmy Barnes sang about "sitting on the beach drinking Rocket Fuel...oh yeah!"

Rusty Nail

Ingredients

Glass: 210mL/7oz Old Fashioned Spirit Glass

Mixers: 30mL/1fl oz Scotch Whisky

30mL/1fl oz Drambuie

Method

Build over ice.

Garnish: Lemon twist (optional).

Comments: A traditional pillow softener for refined gentlemen. The highlands of Scotland's Drambuie ascends your spirit above the centre of the world. Lemon will diffuse the bite of the Scotch. Watch your step when ordering!

Salty Dog

Ingredients

Glass: 285mL/9oz Hi-Ball Glass – Salt-rimmed

Mixers: 45mL/1½fl oz Vodka
               top-up with Grapefruit Juice

Method

Build over ice.

Garnish: Swizzle stick, straws optional.

Comments: Slowly re-emerging as the long cool cocktail it was renowned for in its heyday. Unfortunately, a limited number of bars stock Grapefruit Juice, which restricts availability. But as the saying goes " Every dog has his day". Straws are unnecessary, drink the cocktail from the salt rim.

Sangria

Ingredients

Glass: 180mL/6oz Wine Glass

Mixers: 20mL/²/₃fl oz Cointreau
20mL/²/₃fl oz brandy
20mL/²/₃fl oz Bacardi
orange, lime, lemon and
strawberry pieces
sugar syrup
Spanish Red Wine

Method

Pour in order.

Thinly slice orange and lime and place in bowl. Pour in
sugar syrup and allow to stand for several hours.
Add Red Wine.

Satin Pillow

Ingredients

Glass: 140mL/5oz Cocktail Glass

Mixers: 5mL/1/6fl oz Strawberry Liqueur
10mL/1/3fl oz Cointreau
15mL/1/2fl oz Frangelico
15mL/1/2fl oz Tia Maria
20mL/2/3fl oz Pineapple juice
20mL/2/3fl oz Cream

Method

Blend with ice and pour.

Garnish: Cut a strawberry in half and place on side of glass then swirl cream over strawberry halves.

Comments: The very piquant taste is as smooth as satin bed linen.

Screwdriver

Ingredients

Glass: 210mL/7oz Old Fashioned Spirit Glass

Mixers: 45mL/1½fl oz Vodka
               45mL/1½fl oz Orange juice

Method

Build over ice.

Garnish: Orange twist or spiral.

Comments: A frequently requested basic spirit mixed drink. Subtle at any time of day. The original recipe contains equal measurements of Vodka and Orange Juice.

A Comfortable Screw is made with 30mL Vodka, 15mL Southern Comfort and topped with Orange Juice.

A Slow Comfortable Screw has the addition of 15mL Sloe Gin.

A Long Slow Comfortable Screw is a longer drink served in a 285mL Hi-Ball glass.

A Long Slow Comfortable Screw Up Against A Wall has the addition of 15mL Galliano floated.

Scorpion

Ingredients

Glass: 140mL Cocktail Glass

Mixers: 15mL/½fl oz dark rum
15mL/½fl oz Cognac
15mL/½fl oz sambuca
15mL/½fl oz Orgeat
45mL/1½fl oz orange juice
15mL/½fl oz lemon juice

Method

Blend with ice. Garnish with a lime wheel with cherry.

From the trading capital of the Middle East is where this perilously animal and cocktail comes from! Remember they have a sting in their tail. Orgeat is an almond-flavoured non-alcoholic syrup. Amaretto may be used as a substitute.

Sex on the Beach

Ingredients

Glass: 210mL/7oz Fancy Cocktail Glass

Mixers: 15mL/½fl oz Kahlúa
30mL/1fl oz Malibu
30mL/1fl oz Pineapple Liqueur
60mL/2fl oz Cream

Method

Shake with ice and strain.

Garnish: Pineapple wedge on side of glass.

Comments: A most enjoyable cocktail when you fell mischievous.

Shanghai Punch

Ingredients

Glass: 350mL/12oz Fancy Hi-Ball Glass

Mixers: 30mL/1fl oz cognac

              30mL/1fl oz dark rum

              45mL/1½fl oz orange juice

              20mL/⅔fl oz Cointreau

              20mL/⅔fl oz lemon juice

              almond extract

              fresh tea

              grated orange and lemon peels

              cinnamon sticks

Method

Boil tea and add ingredients then stir.

Sicilian Kiss

Ingredients

Glass: 150mL/5oz Old Fashioned

Mixers: 30mL/1fl oz Southern Comfort

30mL/1fl oz amaretto

Method

Build with ice.

Sidecar

Ingredients

Glass: 90mL/3oz Cocktail Glass

Mixers: 30mL/1fl oz Brandy

20mL/²⁄₃fl oz Cointreau*

30mL/1fl oz Lemon juice

Method

Shake with ice and strain.

Garnish: Lemon twist optional.

Comments: A zappy pre-dinner cocktail. The Lemon juice purifies the brandy and ferments the Cointreau. Too much Lemon Juice will leave an acidic after taste.

*Cointreau may be substituted with Triple Sec.

Snowball

Ingredients

Glass: 285mL/9oz Hi-ball Glass

Mixers: 30mL/1fl oz Advocaat Liqueur
Top-up with Lemonade
Dash of Lime Cordial
Cream, optional

Method

Build over ice.

Garnish: Red cherry. Swizzle sticks and straws.

Comments: Place ice in the glass after mixing the Advocaat with Lemonade before floating cream on top. The pressure of a post mix gun will create the desired 'snowball' effect.

South Pacific

Ingredients

Glass: 285mL/9oz Hi-ball Glass

Mixers: 30mL/1fl oz Dry Gin

              15mL/¹⁄₂fl oz Galliano

              top with Lemonade

              15mL/¹⁄₂fl oz Blue Curacao Liqueur

Method

Build over ice, then add the Blue Curacao last.

Garnish: Lemon slice and cherry, swizzle stick and straws.

Comments: Australia's first gold medal winning cocktail. Created by Gary Revell, to win the World Cocktail Championships in Yugoslavia in 1979.

Southern Peach

Ingredients

Glass: 140mL/5oz Martini Glass

Mixers: 30mL/1fl oz Cointreau

15mL/½fl oz Brandy

15mL/½fl oz Cherry Brandy Liqueur

15mL/½fl oz Pineapple juice

15mL/½fl oz Lemon juice

Method

Shake with ice and strain.

Garnish: Butterfly a strawberry, place on side of glass, twirl cream over strawberry and sprinkle over flaked chocolate.

Comments: A magical cocktail that can be 'fluffed' up by adding egg white.

Splice

Ingredients

Glass: 210mL/7oz Hurricane Glass

Mixers: 30mL/1fl oz Melon Liqueur
              15mL/½fl oz Galliano
              15mL/½fl oz Coconut Liqueur
              30mL/1fl oz Pineapple juice
              30mL/1fl oz Cream

Method

Blend with ice and pour.

Garnish: Pineapple wedge and leaves on side of glass.

Comments: Enjoyed in Australia for several years. The smooth, well blended flavour has ensured this cocktails ever increasing admiration.

Spritzer

Ingredients

Glass: 185mL/6oz Wine Goblet

Mixers: Dry White Wine, chilled
                    Soda Water

Method

Build, no ice.

Garnish: None.

Comments: "Wet the whistle" with a responsible alcoholic alternative. Ladies prefer the soda dilution although you may be asked for lemonade.

Stars & Stripes

Ingredients

Glass: 300mL/10oz Fancy Cocktail Glass

Mixers: 10mL/⅓fl oz Blue Curacao
Blender 1
30mL/1fl oz Southern Comfort
30mL/1fl oz Frangelico
Blender 2
30mL/1fl oz Strawberry Liqueur
3-4 Strawberries

Method

Pour Blue Curacao into glass. Blend other ingredients with ice in 2 separate blenders and pour.

Garnish: Sprinkle grated chocolate flakes over top and add a strawberry and USA flag to side of glass.

Comments: Remember to tilt the glass when pouring the two sets of ingredients. A refreshingly super-powered alcoholic cocktail without juice.

Stinger

Ingredients
Glass: 90mL/3oz Cocktail Glass
Mixers: 45mL/1½fl oz Brandy
                10mL/⅓fl oz White Crème de Menthe

Method
Stir over ice and strain.
Garnish: None.

Comments: The distinct minty aroma of White Crème de Menthe prevades this prefect pre-dinner cocktail. The Brandy delivers the sting!

Strawberry Blonde

Ingredients

Glass: 285mL/9oz Hi-Ball Glass

Mixers: 30mL/1fl oz Dark Creme de Cacao
top-up with cola
fresh cream, floated
splash of Grenadine

Method

Build over ice.

Garnish: A red cherry. Swizzle sticks and straws.

Comments: Tasting this cocktail will reveal the secret why
'blondes have more fun'. Placing ice in the glass after mixing
the Carao with Cola will support the floating cream on top.
A dessert cocktail. Ideal on a blind date.

Summer Breeze

Ingredients

Glass: 300mL/10oz Fancy Cocktail Glass
Mixers: 60mL/2oz Peach Tree Liqueur
15mL/½fl oz Rum
15mL/½fl oz Mango Liqueur
15mL/½fl oz Gin
60mL/2fl oz Pineapple juice
60mL/2fl oz Orange juice
1 fresh Mango
1 fresh Peach

Method

Blend with ice and pour.
Garnish: Half an orange slice and orange peel twist.
Comments: A glorious cocktail slurped on the Great Barrier Reef. With temperature hot and humidity high, this is often the only summer breeze available in the afternoon.

Sunken Treasure

Ingredients

Glass: 90mL/3oz Cocktail Glass

Mixers: 30mL/1fl oz Gin
15mL/½fl oz Peach Liqueur
Champagne to top-up
apricot conserve

Method

Stir over ice, strain and top-up.

Garnish: Place a teaspoon of apricot conserve in the bottom of glass and then push a strawberry into conserve.

Comments: It is always pleasing to include innovative cocktail garnishes. Stir Gin and Peach Liqueur over ice and strain, then top glass with champagne. 1989 Australian National Cocktail winner.

Swedish Snowball

Ingredients

Glass: 210mL/7oz Old Fashioned

Mixers: 30mL/1fl oz advocaat

15mL/½fl oz lemon juice

top up with soda water

Method

Build over ice then top up with soda.
Garnish with a lemon slice.

Sweet Lady Jane

Ingredients

Glass: 140mL/5oz Champagne Saucer

Mixers: 15mL/½fl oz Grand Marnier
15mL/½fl oz Orange Juice
15mL/½fl oz Cointreau
15mL/½fl oz Coconut Cream
30mL/1fl oz Strawberry Liqueur
30mL/1fl oz fresh cream

Method

Shake with ice and strain.

Garnish: Strawberry, mint and chocolate flakes.

Comments: An orange glazed cocktail gorgeously presented with chocolate flakes that swirl the coconut and strawberry liqueurs.

Sweet Martini

Ingredients

Glass: 90mL/3oz Cocktail Glass

Mixers: 45mL/1½fl oz Dry Gin

              20ml/⅔fl oz Rosso Vermouth

Method

Stir over ice and strain.

Garnish: Red cherry on toothpick in glass.

Comments: Sister to the "Dry Martini", the sweeter Vermouth overwhelms the Gin sting. A pre-dinner cocktail which can be stirred and strained either:

"On The Rocks" - served in a standard Spirit glass over ice.

"Straight Up" - served in a 90mL/3oz Cocktail Glass over ice.

Tequila Slammer

Ingredients

Glass: 185mL/6oz Old Fashioned Spirit glass

Mixers: 30mL/1fl oz Tequila
60mL/2fl oz Dry Ginger Ale

Method

Build, no ice.

Garnish: None.

Comments: A one hit wonder - holding a coaster over the entire rim, rotate the glass clockwise on the bar 4-5 times.

Lift and 'slam' the base of the glass down onto the bar, then skol in one shot. The carbonated mixer fizzes the Tequila when slammed.

Usually bartenders just use a splash of Dry Ginger Ale to aid the quick drinking process.

Tequila Sunrise

Ingredients

Glass: 285mL/9oz Hi-Ball Glass

Mixers: 30mL/1fl oz Tequila
5mL/⅙fl oz Grenadine
top-up with Orange juice

Method

Build over ice.

Garnish: Orange wheel, a red cherry.
Swizzle stick and straws.

Comments: Sipping this long cool cocktail at sunrise or sunset is magnificient.

To obtain the cleanest visual effect, drop Grenadine down the inside of the glass, after topping up with Orange Juice. Dropping Grenadine in the middle creates a fallout effect, detracting from the presentation of the cocktail.

Best served with chilled, freshly squeezed oranges.

The Dik Hewett

Ingredients

Glass: 140mL/5oz Cocktail Glass

Mixers: 30mL/1fl oz Jack Daniel's Old No. 7
30mL/1fl oz Cognac
30mL/1fl oz Benedictine
glass of water (on the side)

Method

Shake with ice and strain.

Garnish: None

Comments: The late arrival cocktail. Sure to test, sure to please.

T.N.T.

Ingredients

Glass: 90mL/3oz Cocktail Glass

Mixers: 45mL/1½fl oz Brandy
20mL/⅔fl oz Orange Liqueur
dash of Pernod
dash of Angostura Bitters

Method

Stir over ice and strain.

Garnish: Orange twist.

Comments: A powder keg, really a cocktail to liven up the party. Drink in moderation, as this one can really cause a "bang".

Toblerone

Ingredients

Glass: 140mL/5oz Cocktail Glass

Mixers: 5mL/⅙fl oz Baileys Irish Cream
15mL/½fl oz Kahlúa
15mL/½fl oz White Creme de Cacao
30mL/1fl oz Frangelico
60mL/2fl oz Cream
½ teaspoon Honey

Method

Blend with ice and pour.

Garnish: Sprinkle almond flakes and nutmeg over top. To create a special effect drag a cotton strand over completed cocktail.

Comments: A favourite at Melbourne's Collins Street exclusive 5 star cocktail bars. Accompanying chocolates make this cocktail bliss before the theatre.

Tom Collins

Ingredients

Glass: 140mL Champagne Saucer

Mixers: 60mL/2fl oz lemon juice
60mL/2fl oz gin
soda water

Method

Put cracked ice, lemon juice, soda water and gin in a glass. Fill with soda water and stir. Serve with a slice of lemon and cherry for garnish.

Brandy, bourbon, rum or any whisky can be used instead of gin, the Collins is named after the liqour used, eg. Rum Collins.

Trader Vic's Rum Fizz

Ingredients

Glass: 135mL/4½ oz Tulip Champagne Glass

Mixers: 30mL/1fl oz dark rum

30mL/1fl oz lemon juice

10mL/⅓fl oz sugar

15mL/½fl oz cream soda

1 raw egg

Method

Shake over ice and pour. Garnish with an orange spiral.

From the range of cocktails for which the internationally renowned cocktail bar proprietor has become recognised.

Tropical Itch

Ingredients

Glass: 425mL/14oz Hurricane Glass

Mixers: 45mL/1½fl oz Rum
45mL/1½fl oz Bourbon
juice of half fresh lime
dash Angostura Bitters
top-up with pineapple juice and passionfruit
30mL/1fl oz Rum, floated

Method

Build over ice.
Garnish: Pineapple spear, mint and cherry plus wooden backscratcher and straws.

Comments: When you're troubled with an itching-tickling throat, delight in this spectacularly garnished fruity coctail. A proven quenching recipe after sunbaking. The name is derived from the inclusion of the backscratcher.

Voodoo Child

Ingredients

Glass: 90mL/3oz Cocktail Glass

Mixers: 15mL/1/2fl oz Melon Liqueur
15mL/1/2fl oz Black Sambuca
15mL/1/2fl oz Baileys Irish Cream
15mL/1/2fl oz Tia Maria
15mL/1/2fl oz cream

Method

Layer Melon Liqueur on Black Sambuca in glass. Shake other ingredients with ice and strain.

Garnish: Green and black jelly babies on a skewer, then place across top of glass.

Comments: Scare yourself with this novel cocktail. It's a fun filled cocktail guaranteed to lift any spell.

Whisky Sour

Ingredients

Glass: 140mL/5oz Wine Glass

Mixers: 45mL/1½fl oz Scotch Whisky
30mL/1fl oz Lemon Juice
15mL/½fl oz Sugar syrup
½ Egg white

Method

Shake with ice and strain.

Garnish: Red cherry at bottom of glass and slice of lemon on side.

Comment: A quaint appetiser before dinner. Shake vigorously so the egg white rises to a frothy head after straining. Some people prefer a 140mL/5oz Coctail glass.

White Lady

Ingredients

Glass: 90mL/3oz Cocktail Glass

Mixers: 30mL/1fl oz Dry Gin
15mL/½fl oz Lemon Juice
15mL/½fl oz Sugar Syrup
½ Egg White

Method

Shake with ice and strain.

Garnish: Twist of lemon.

Comments: a traditional pre-dinner cocktail. Pure yet bland, change to either: "Blue Lady" - substitute Blue Curacao for sugar syrup. "Pink Lady" - substitute Grenadine for sugar syrup and add cream.

Widow's Kiss

Ingredients

Glass: 90mL/3oz Cocktail Glass

Mixers: 30mL/1fl oz apple brandy
10mL/⅓fl oz Benedictine
10mL/⅓fl oz yellow Chartreuse
5mL/⅙fl oz Angostura Bitters

Method

Shake over ice and strain. Garnish with a floating strawberry.

Woodstock

Ingredients

Glass: 150mL/5oz Old Fashioned spirit glass, sugar rimmed with maple syrup

Mixers: 30mL/1fl oz gin
10mL/⅓fl oz lemon juice
10mL/⅓fl oz maple syrup
2 dashes Angostura Bitters

Method

Shake over ice and strain then add cubed ice.

X.T.C.

Ingredients

Glass: 90mL/3oz Cocktail Glass

Mixers: 30mL/1fl oz Tia Maria
30mL/1fl oz Strawberry Liqueur
30mL/1fl oz Cream

Method

Shake with ice and strain.

Garnish: Butterfly strawberry placed on side of glass, twirl thickened cream over strawberry and sprinkle over flaked chocolate.

Comments: X-rated, tall and cute! Enjoy a truly enjoyable Ectasy before you dance all night long.

Zombie

Ingredients

Glass: 300mL/10oz Fancy Cocktail Glass

Mixers: 40mL/1¹/₃fl oz Bacardi*
30mL/1fl oz Dark Rum
30mL/1fl oz Light Rum
30mL/1fl oz Pineapple Juice
15mL/¹/₂fl oz Lime or Lemon Juice
30mL/1fl oz Apricot Brandy
5mL/¹/₆fl oz sugar syrup

Method

Shake with ice and pour.

Garnish: Pineapple spear and leaves, cherry and mint leaves, swizzle stick and straws.

Comments: A well-known Hawaiian cocktail. Resurrect youself with this supernatural Rum-A-Thon cocktail. It is usually the last recipe on cocktail lists.

After Eight

Ingredients

Glass: Cordial (Embassy)

Mixers: 10mL/⅓fl oz Kahlúa

10mL/⅓fl oz Creme de Menthe

20mL/⅔fl oz Baileys Irish Cream

15mL/½fl oz Southern Comfort

Method

Pour in order.

Technique: Shoot

Comments: A peppermint surprise.

Atomic Bomb

Ingredients

Glass: Tall Dutch Cordial

Mixers: 20mL/²/₃fl oz Tia Maria

15mL/¹/₂fl oz Gin

10mL/¹/₃fl oz cream

Method

Layer in order, then float cream.

Technique: Shoot

Comments: A strategic 'one shooter weapon', this drink explodes down the unsuspecting throat. Delicious in emergencies! Gin may be replaced with Cointreau, or Triple Sec.

B&B Shooter

Ingredients

Glass: Cordial (Lexington)

Mixers: One part Cognac or Brandy
One part DOM Benedictine

Method

Pour in order.

Technique: Shoot.

Comments: For mature drinkers! Grandpa can turn up the pace of his medication. The shooter is quick and smooth, the traditional B & B cocktail is normally served in a brandy balloon.

Banana Split

Ingredients

Glass: Tall Dutch Cordial

Mixers: 15mL/¹/₂fl oz Kahlúa

           15mL/¹/₂fl oz Lena Banana Liqueur

           10mL/¹/₃fl oz Strawberry Liqueur

           Whipped Cream

Method

Layer in order and top with whipped cream.

Technique: Shoot

Comments: Let this one slip down sweetly, with a super strawberry aftertaste.

Bee Sting

Ingredients

Glass: Cordial (Embassy)

Mixers: 20mL/²/₃fl oz Tequila

10mL/¹/₃fl oz Yellow Chartreuse

Method

Layer in order, then light.

Technique: Straw shoot while flaming.

Comments: Ouch! The Yellow Chartreuese attacks your throat with a numbing, pleasurable pain, as Tequila buzzes you back to the party. Drink quickly so the straw won't melt!

Black Nuts

Ingredients

Glass: Corzdial (Embassy)

Mixers: 15mL/¹⁄₂fl oz Black Sambucca
                15mL/¹⁄₂fl oz Frangelico

Method

Layer in order.

Technique: Shoot.

Comments: A wonderful "nutty" flavour, with a real anise touch.

Black Widow

Ingredients

Glass: Cordial (Embassy)

Mixers: 10mL/¹/₃fl oz Strawberry Liqueur

              10mL/¹/₃fl oz Black Sambuca

              10mL/¹/₃fl ozcream

Method

Layer in order.

Technique: Shoot

Comments: Watch this one, the spider will get you quickly

Blood Bath

Ingredients

Glass: Whisky Shot

Mixers: 10mL/¹/₃fl oz Rosso Vermouth

                      15mL/¹/₃fl oz Strawberry Liqueur

                      20mL/²/₃fl oz Tequila

Method

Pour in order then layer the Tequila.

Technique: Shoot.

Comments: Cherry grins and rosy cheeks characterise the after effects of this blood thirsty experience. Only issued after midnight and before dawn.

Blow Job

Ingredients

Glass: Tall Dutch Cordial

Mixers: Two parts Kahlúa
One part Baileys Irish Cream

Method

Layer in order and shoot.

Technique: Shoot

Comments: A light minty confectionery flavour and creamy texture provide a mouthful for those who indulge.

Twist this to a **"Rattlesnake"** by adding Green Chartreuse.

Brain Damage

Ingredients

Glass: Cordial (Lexington)

Mixers: 20mL/²⁄₃fl oz Coconut Liqueur
10mL/¹⁄₃fl oz Parfait Amour Liqueur
5mL/¹⁄₆fl oz Advocaat Liqueur

Method

Layer the Parfait Amour and Coconut Liqueur, then pour the Advocaat.

Technique: Shoot.

Comments: Separation induces restless nights. Advocaat intervenes to mould the senses.

Brave Bull

Ingredients

Glass: Whiskey Shot

Mixers: 30mL/1fl oz Crème de Café Liqueur

15mL/½fl oz Tequila

Method

Layer in order.

Technique: Shoot

Comments: One of my favourites for late night revellers, will resist fatique and maintain stamina. Ad Ouzo and a "TKO" is punched out.

Candy Cane

Ingredients

Glass: Tall Dutch Cordial

Mixers: 15mL/½fl oz Grenadine Cordial
15mL/½fl oz Creme de Menthe
25mL/⅚fl oz Vodka

Method

Layer in order and shoot.

Technique: Shoot

Comments: A real candy flavour, with a touch of menthol.

Chastity Belt

Ingredients

Glass: Tall Dutch Cordial

Mixers: 20mL/²⁄₃fl oz Tia Maria

10mL/¹⁄₃fl oz Frangelico

10mL/¹⁄₃fl oz Baileys Irish Cream

5mL/¹⁄₆fl oz Cream

Method

Layer in order, then float the cream.

Technique: Shoot

Comments: Morality implores you not to succumb to the super-sweet delicacies of drinking's perversity.

Chilli Shot

Ingredients

Glass: Whisky Shot

Mixers: 45mL/1½fl oz Vodka

Slice of red chilli pepper

Method

Pour.

Technique: Shoot.

Comments: Feeling mischievous? Refrigerate the Vodka with one red chilli pepper (or 3 to 5 drops of Tabasco sauce) for 24 hours before serving.

Chocolate Nougat

Ingredients

Glass: Cordial (Embassy)

Mixers: 10mL/⅓fl oz Frangelico Hazelnut Liqueur
10mL/⅓fl oz DOM Benedictine
10mL/⅓fl oz Baileys Irish Cream

Method

Pour in order then layer the Bailey's Irish Cream.

Technique: Shoot

Comments: A swirling pleasure zone of flowing Bailey's Irish Cream, above the finest Benedictine and based with voluptuous hazelnuts, accentuating the meaning of chocolate.

Coathanger

Ingredients

Glass: Cordial (Lexington)

Mixers: 15mL/¹/₂fl oz Cointreau*
15mL/¹/₂fl oz Tequila
7mL/¹/₄fl oz Grenadine cordial
drop of milk

Method

Layer Tequila onto the Cointreau, dash Cordial or Grenadine then drop the milk.

Techniqzue: Shoot, then cup hand entirely over the rim, insert straw between fingers into the glass and inhale fumes.

Comments: A euphoric experience, quiet stunning to your senses.

* Cointreau may be replaced with Triple Sec Liqueur.

Courting Penelope

Ingredients

Glass: Cordial (Lexington)

Mixers: 20mL/²/₃fl oz Cognac
15mL/¹/₂fl oz Grand Marnier

Method

Pour in order

Technique: Shoot.

Comments: *A distinctive acquired taste is needed for two inseparable moments!*

Dark Sunset

Ingredients

Glass: Tall Dutch Cordial

Mixers: One part Dark Crème de Cacao Liqueur
                 One part Malibu

Method

Layer in order.

Technique: Shoot.

Comments: This tropical paradise reflects sunset, beaches and the ripe coconuts of Malibu.

Devil's Handbrake

Ingredients

Glass: Tall Dutch Cordial

Mixers: 15mL/½fl oz Banana Liqueur

              15mL/½fl oz Mango Liqueur

              15mL/½fl oz Cherry Brandy

Method

Layer in order.

Technique: Shoot

Comments: A magnificent bounty off fruit infiltrated by the devil. Exquisite after a swim.

Dirty Orgasm

Ingredients

Glass: Tall Dutch Cordial

Mixers: 15mL/½fl oz Triple Sec Liqueur

15mL/½fl oz Galliano

15mL/½fl oz Baileys Irish Cream

Method

Layer in order.

Technique: Shoot.

Comments: The Irish frolic between the world's two best lovers, Italian Galliano and French Cointreau. Also known as a **"Screaming Orgasm"**. Drambuie may replace Galliano.

Double Date

Ingredients

Glass: Tall Dutch Cordial

Mixers: 15mL/½fl oz Melon Liqueur
15mL/½fl oz White Crème de Menthe
15mL/½fl oz DOM Benedictine

Method

Layer in order.

Technique: Tandem.

Comments: Soothing Crème de Menthe restrains the passion of DOM and Melon. For romantics.

Face Off

Ingredients

Glass: Tall Dutch Cordial

Mixers: 10mL/⅓fl oz Grenadine

15mL/½fl oz Creme de Menthe

10mL/⅓fl oz Parfait Amour

10mL/⅓fl oz Sambuca

Method

Layer in order.

Technique: Shoot

Comments: Too many of these will certainly cause a loss of face.

Fizzy Rush

Ingredients

Glass: Tall Dutch Cordial

Mixers: 5mL/⅙fl oz White Crème de Menthe

                 10mL/⅓fl oz Apricot Brandy

                 30mL/1fl oz Champagne

Method

Pour in order.

Technique: Shoot.

Comments: Bubbles of refreshing Apricot guaranteed to get up your nose.

Flaming Lamborghini Shooter

Ingredients

Glass: Cordial (Embassy)

Mixers: 10mL/⅓fl oz Crème de Café Liqueur
10mL/⅓fl oz Galliano
10mL/⅓fl oz Green Chartreuse

Method

Layer in order, then light.

Technique: Shoot while flaming.

Comments: Get the party into motion. Essential for birthday celebrants.

Flaming Lover

Ingredients

Glass: Cordial (Embassy)

Mixers: 15mL/½fl oz Sambuca

15mL/½fl oz Triple Sec Liqueur

Method

Pour Triple Sec over lit Sambuca while drinking through a straw.

Technique: Straw shoot while flaming.

Comments: The Triple Sec softens the flame for inexperienced drinkers of flaming shooters.

Flaming Orgy

Ingredients

Glass: Tall Dutch Cordial

Mixers: 10mL/¹⁄₃fl oz Grenadine
10mL/¹⁄₃fl oz Creme de Menthe
15mL/¹⁄₂fl oz Brandy
10mL/¹⁄₃fl oz Tequila

Method

Technique: Straw shoot while flaming.

Comments: Another of the potent flaming shooters. Don't get your lips too close to this one.

Flaming Sambuca

Ingredients

Glass: Cordial (Embassy)

Mixers: 30mL/1fl oz Sambuca

3 Coffee Beans

Method

Pour Sambuca, float coffee beans and light.

Technique: Shoot after flame extinguished.

Comments: Provides relief from the cold winter. The other way we do it, is to pour Sambuca into a sine glass then light. Cup your hand entirely over the rim while it flames, creating suction. Shake the glass, place under your nose, take your hand from the glass to inhale the fumes, then shoot!

Freddie Fud Pucker

Ingredients

Glass: Cordial (Lexington)

Mixers: 22mL/²/₃fl oz Galliano

10mL/¹/₃fl oz Tequila

5mL/¹/₆fl oz Orange Curacao Liqueur

Method

Layer Tequila onto Galliano then drop Orange Curacao.

Technique: Shoot.

Comments: Known to induce dancing on bars and at beach parties, be sure to mind you 'p's and f's' when ordering.

Fruit Tingle

Ingredients

Glass: Cordial (Embassy)

Mixers: 10mL/¹/₃fl oz Blue Curacao Liqueur
15mL/¹/₂fl oz Mango Liqueur
5mL/¹/₆fl oz Lemon Juice

Method

Layer in order, optional to stir.

Technique: Shoot.

Comments: Tangy and piquant. Melon Liqueur may be substituted for Mango Liqueur.

Galliano Hot Shot

Ingredients

Glass: Galliano Shot Glass

Mixers: 15mL/½fl oz Galliano

25mL/⅚fl oz Black Coffee

5mL/½fl oz Cream

Method

Top Galliano with black coffee, then float cream.

Technique: Shoot.

Comments: When in a hurry, a great way to enjoy a liqueur coffee.

Golden Cadillac Shooter

Ingredients

Glass: Tall Dutch Cordial

Mixers: 15mL/½fl oz White Crème de Cacao
20mL/⅔fl oz Galliano
10mL/⅓fl oz Cream

Method

Layer Galliano and White Crème de Cacao, then float cream.

Technique: Shoot.

Comments: Comfort in style is what the distilled cocoa beams give golden Galliano - a real dazzler! The traditional Golden Cadillac cocktail has a larger volume, is shaken over ice and served in a 140mL/5oz Champagne Saucer.

Grand Slam

Ingredients

Glass: Cordial (Embassy)

Mixers: 10mL/¹⁄₃fl oz Lena Banana Liqueur
10mL/¹⁄₃fl oz Baileys Irish Cream
10mL/¹⁄₃fl oz Grand Marnier

Method

Pour in order, then stir.

Technique: Shoot

Comments: Add more egg white for greater slime. Melon will keep the taste buds occupied, Vodka dilutes the egg white.

Green Slime

Ingredients

Glass: Whiskey Shot

Mixers: 20mL/²⁄₃fl oz Melon Liqueur
15mL/¹⁄₂fl oz Vodka
5mL/¹⁄₆fl oz Egg White

Method

Pour in order, then stir.

Technique: Shoot.

Comments: Add more egg white for greater slime.
Melon will keep the taste buds occupied, Vodka dilutes the egg white.

Half Nelson

Ingredients

Glass: Whiskey Shot

Mixers: 15mL/½fl oz Crème de Menthe Liqueur
10mL/⅓fl oz Strawberry Liqueur
20mL/⅔fl oz Grand Marnier

Method

Layer in order.

Technique: Shoot.

Comments: The referee is unable to break the grip of Strawberry locking its green opponent into an immovable position. For the temporarily incapacitated.

Harbour Lights

Ingredients

Glass: Cordial (Lexington)

Mixers: 12mL/¹/₃fl oz Kahlúa

             12mL/¹/₃fl oz Sambuca

             12mL/¹/₃fl oz Green Chartreuse

Method

Layer in order.

Technique: Straw shoot.

Comments: Glittering reflections sparkle on the habour beside a candlelight dinner. Substitute Yellow Chartreuse if preferred.

Hard On

Ingredients

Glass: Cordial (Lexington)

Mixers: 20mL/²/₃fl oz Creme de Cafe Liqueur
15mL/½fl oz Banana Liqueur
10mL/¹/₃fl oz Cream

Method

Layer Liqueur onto Kahlua, then float the cream.

Technique: Shoot

Comments: The first to float cream, voted the most popular shooter.

Hellraiser

Ingredients

Glass: Whisky Shot

Mixers: 15mL/½fl oz Melon Liqueur

15mL/½fl oz Strawberry Liqueur

15mL/½fl oz Black Sambuca

Method

Layer in order.

Technique: Shoot

Comments: A hell of a drink!

High and Dry

Ingredients

Glass: Cordial (Embassy)

Mixers: 10mL/⅓fl oz Bianco Vermouth

15mL/½fl oz Tequila

5mL/⅙fl oz Dry Vermouth

Method

Pour in order, then stir.

Technique: Shoot.

Comments: Disguise the mischief of Tequila with Dry Vermouth. Best served chilled.

Inkahlúarable

Ingredients

Glass: Cordial (Embassy)

Mixers: 10mL/⅓fl oz Kahlua

                10mL/⅓fl oz Triple Sec Liqueur

                10mL/⅓fl oz Grand Marnier

Method

Layer in order.

Technique: Shoot.

Comments: Terminal illness can be momentarily postponed with this Kahlua-based antidote.

Irish Flag

Ingredients

Glass: Cordial (Lexington)

Mixers: 12mL/⅓fl oz Green Creme de Menthe
12mL/⅓fl oz Baileys Irish Cream
12mL/⅓fl oz Brandy

Method

Layer in order.

Technique: Shoot

Comments: A stroll through verdant pastures. Brandy may be replaced with Tullamore Dew-an Old Irish Whisky.

Italian Stallion

Ingredients

Glass: Cordial (Lexington)

Mixers: 15mL/¹/₂fl oz Banana Liqueur
15mL/¹/₂fl oz Galliano
7mL/¹/₅fl oz cream

Method

Pour Galliano onto Banana Liqueur, then float cream.
Optional to stir.

Technique: Shoot

Comments: *This creamy banana ride you won't forget.*

Japanese Slipper

Ingredients

Glass: Tall Dutch Cordial

Mixers: 20mL/²⁄₃fl oz Melon Liqueur

                    15mL/¹⁄₂fl oz Triple Sec Liqueur*

                    10mL/¹⁄₃fl oz Lemon Juice

Method

Layer Triple Sec onto the Melon then float the Lemon Juice.
Optional to stir.

Technique: Shoot.

Comments: *Elegant and refreshing. Precision is required
with measurements. To revive failing confidence and
replenish that special feeling.*

Cointreau may be substituted for Triple Sec.

Jawbreaker

Ingredients

Glass: Whisky Shot

Mixers: 45mL/1½fl oz Apricot Brandy

                      4-5 drops Tabasco Sauce

Method

Pour Apricot Brandy then drop Tabasco Sauce.

Technique: Shoot.

Comments: grit your teeth after this shot, then slowly open your mouth.

Jellyfish

Ingredients

Glass: Cordial (Lexington)

Mixers: 10mL/⅓fl oz Blue Curacao Liqueur

10mL/⅓fl oz Romana Sambuca

10mL/⅓fl oz Baileys Irish Cream

2 dashes of Grenadine

Method

Layer in order and pour Grenadine.

Technique: Shoot.

Comments: Watch out for sting at the end of this slippery shooter.

Jumping Jack Flash

Ingredients

Glass: Whisky Shot

Mixers: 15mL/½fl oz Tia Maria

15mL/½fl oz Rum

15mL/½fl oz Jack Daniel's

Method

Layer in order.

Technique: Shoot.

Comments: Thrill seeking Jack Daniel's and his accomplices await this opportunity to shudder your soul.

Jumping Mexican

Ingredients

Glass: Whisky Shot

Mixers: 22mL/²/₃fl oz Crème de Café Liqueur
                      22mL/²/₃fl oz Bourbon

Method

Layer in order.

Technique: Shoot

Comments: Jump into Mexico's favourite pastime and bounce back into the party. For those keen on the Mexican Hat Dance.

Kamikaze Shooter

Ingredients

Glass: Whisky Shot

Mixers: 20mL/²/₃fl oz Vodka

15mL/¹/₂fl oz Cointreau

10mL/¹/₃fl oz Lemon Juice

Method

Layer the Cointreau onto Vodka, float the lemon juice, then optional to stir.

Technique: Shoot

Comments: Maintain freshness for large volumes by adding strained egg white. Mix in a jug and keep refridgerated.

The traditional Kamikaze cocktail has the additional of Lime cordial, it is shaken over ice, strained and then served in a 140mL/5oz Cocktail Glass.

▪Triple Sec may be substituted for Cointreau.

K.G.B. Shooter

Ingredients

Glass: Cordial (Lexington)

Mixers: 12mL/⅓fl oz Kahlua

                  12mL/⅓fl oz Grand Marnier

                  12mL/⅓fl oz Baileys Irish Cream

Method

Layer in order.

Technique: Shoot.

Comments: Grand Marnier adds an orange twist to the Kahlua and Baileys Irish Cream. The traditional K.G.B. cocktail is built over ice with greater volume of ingredient. It is normally served in a 140mL/5oz Old Fashioned Spirit Glass.

Kool Aid

Ingredients

Glass: Cordial (Lexington)

Mixers: 10mL/⅓fl oz Melon Liqueur
                 15mL/½fl oz Amaretto di Saroono
                 10mL/⅓fl oz Vodka

Method

Layer in order.

Technique: Shoot.

Comments: A familiar mix with various names. Amaretto's caramel lacing prevents overheating.

Lady Throat Killer

Ingredients

Glass: Tall Dutch Cordial

Mixers: 20mL/²⁄₃fl oz Crème de Café Liqueur

                15mL/¹⁄₂fl oz Melon Liqueur

                10mL/¹⁄₃fl oz Frangelico Hazelnut Liqueur

Method

Layer in order.

Technique: Shoot.

Comments: This superb mixture offers an exquisite after-taste. One of my favourite Shooters.

Lambada

Ingredients

Glass: Whisky Shot

Mixers: 15mL/½fl oz Mango Liqueur

              15mL/½fl oz Black Sambuca

              15mL/½fl oz Tequila

Method

Layer in order.

Technique: Shoot.

Comments: Wiggle your way to the bar and order the latest liqueur, Black Sambuca. Both the dance and the Shooter will excite your partner.

Laser Beam

Ingredients

Glass: Tall Dutch Cordial

Mixers: 25mL/⁵/₆fl oz Galliano

20mL/²/₃fl oz Tequila

Method

Layer in order and shoot.

Technique: Shoot

Comments: Your palate is illuminated on this celestial journey!

Lick Sip Suck

Ingredients

Glass: Whisky Shot

Mixers: 30mL/1fl oz Tequila
lemon in quarters or slices
salt

Method

Pour Tequila into glass. On the flat piece of skin between the base of your thumb and index finger, place a pinch of salt. Place a quarter of the lemon by you on the bar. Lick the salt off your hand, shoot the Tequila and then suck the lemon in quick succession.

Marc's Rainbow

Ingredients

Glass: Whisky Shot

Mixers: 8mL/¹⁄₅fl oz Crème de Café Liqueur
8mL/¹⁄₅fl oz Melon Liqueur
8mL/¹⁄₅fl oz Malibu
8mL/¹⁄₅fl oz Banana Liqueur
8mL/¹⁄₅fl oz Galliano
8mL/¹⁄₅fl oz Grand Marnier

Method

Layer in order.

Technique: Shoot.

Comments: One of Melbourne's best shooter recipes. Discover the pot of gold at the end of the rainbow.

Margarita Shooter

Ingredients

Glass: Whisky Shot

Mixers: 15mL/½fl oz Cointreau*
               15mL/½fl oz Tequila
               10mL/⅓fl oz Lemon Juice
               5mL/⅙fl oz Lime Juice

Method

Layer Tequila onto Cointreau, float lemon juice then dash the lime juice.

Technique: Shoot.

Comments: Everyone should take this plunge. Lemon and Lime neutralise the acid. This Shooter is similar to the traditional Margarita cocktail, which is of greater volume, shaken over ice and served in a salt rimmed Champagne Saucer.

*Triple Sec may be substituted for Cointreau.

Martian Hard On

Ingredients

Glass: Tall Dutch Cordial

Mixers: 15mL/¹/₂fl oz Dark Crème de Cacao
                    15mL/¹/₂fl oz Melon Liqueur
                    15mL/¹/₂fl oz Baileys Irish Cream

Method

Layer in order.

Technique: Shoot.

Comments: When you are a little green about the facts of life.

Melon Splice

Ingredients

Glass: Tall Dutch Cordial

Mixers: 15mL/½fl oz Melon Liqueur

                 15mL/½fl oz Galliano

                 15mL/½fl oz Coconut Liqueur

Method

Layer in order.

Technique: Shoot.

Comments: Synonymous with Sunday strolls and ice-cream. Flakes of ice may be sprinkled to chill.

Mexican Flag

Ingredients

Glass: Tall Dutch Cordial

Mixers: 15mL/½fl oz Grenadine Cordial

15mL/½fl oz Creme de Menthe

15mL/½fl oz Tequila

Method

Layer in order and shoot.

Technique: Shoot

Comments: Try this "South of the Border" flag waver.

Nude Bomb

Ingredients

Glass: Cordial (Embassy)

Mixers: 10mL/⅓fl oz Kahlúa

            10mL/⅓fl oz Banana Liqueur

            10mL/⅓fl oz Amaretto di Saronno

Method

Layer in order.

Technique: Shoot

Comments: Especially created for toga-parties and skinny-dipping.

Orgasm Shooter

Ingredients

Glass: Whisky Shot

Mixers: One part Coinreau*

                    One part Baileys Irish Cream

Method

Layer in order.

Technique: Shoot.

Comments: After the first one, you most certainly will want another. The Shooter method is different to the traditional Orgasm cocktail, which is a linger drink, built over ice and served in a 210mL/7oz Old Fashioned Spirit Glass.

*Triple Sec may be substituted for Cointreau.

Oyster Shooter

Ingredients

Glass: Cordial (Embassy)

Mixers: 10mL/¹⁄₃fl oz Vodka

                          10mL/¹⁄₃fl oz Tomato Juice

                          5mL/¹⁄₆fl oz Cocktail Sauce (see page 10)

                          Worcestershire sauce to taste

                          Tabasco sauce to taste

                          1 fresh oyster

Method

Pour tomato juice onto the Vodka, float the cocktail sauce, dash sauces to taste and drop in oyster.

Technique: Shoot.

Comments: An early morning wake-up call, replenishing energy lost the night before. Also referred to as a Heart Starter.

Passion Juice

Ingredients

Glass: Whisky Shot

Mixers: 20mL/²/₃fl oz Orange Curacao Liqueur
10mL/¹/₃fl oz Cherry Brandy Liqueur
15mL/¹/₂fl oz freshly squeezed Orange
or Lemon juice

Method

Layer in order. Optional to stir.

Technique: Shoot.

Comments: A bitter sweet lift by garnishing liqueur passion with juices.

Peach Tree Bay

Ingredients

Glass: Tall Dutch Cordial

Mixers: 25mL/⅚fl oz Peachtree Schnapps

15mL/½fl oz Pimm's No. 1 Cup

5mL/⅙fl oz Crème de Menthe Liqueur

Method

Layer the Pimm's onto the Peachtree Schnapps, then drop Green Crème de Menthe.

Technique: Shoot.

Comments: Conjuring an image of uninhabited places, cool refreshing Pimm's is minted with Green Crème de Menthe

Peachy Bum

Ingredients

Glass: Tall Dutch Cordial

Mixers: 20mL/²/₃fl oz Mango Liqueur

                    15mL/½fl oz Peachtree Schnapps

                    10mL/⅓fl oz Cream

Method

Layer in order.

Technique: Shoot.

Comments: Delightfully enriched and mellowed by fresh cream.

Pearl Necklace

Ingredients

Glass: Cordial (Embassy)

Mixers: 15mL/½fl oz Melon Liqueur

               15mL/½fl oz Pimm's No. 1 Cup

Method

Layer in order.

Technique: Shoot.

Comments: a dash of lemonade dilutes the zappy after-taste.

Perfect Match

Ingredients

Glass: Cordial (Lexington)

Mixers: 20mL/²/₃fl oz Parfait Amour Liqueur
20mL/²/₃fl ozMalibu

Method

Layer in order.

Technique: Shoot.

Comments: Parfaits (Perfect), Amour (Love), proposes future happiness and togetherness and under Malibu's exotic veil.

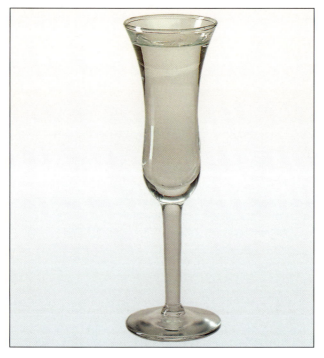

Pipeline

Ingredients

Glass: Tall Dutch Cordial

Mixers: 25mL/⅚fl oz Tequila

20mL/⅔fl oz Vodka

Method

Layer in order.

Technique: Shoot

Comments: Ride the wild surf in this pipeline.

Pipsqueak

Ingredients

Glass: Cordial (Embassy)

Mixers: 20mL/²/₅fl oz Frangelico Hazelnut Liqueur

10mL/¹/₃fl oz Vodka

7mL/¹/₆fl oz Lemon Juice

Method

Layer in order, then stir.

Technique: Shoot.

Comments: Another favourite of mine. A quaint appetiser before dinner.

Rabbit-Punch

Ingredients

Glass: Whisky Shot

Mixers: 10mL/⅓fl oz Campari

                    10mL/⅓fl oz Dark Crème de Cacao

                    10mL/⅓fl oz Malibu

                    15mL/½fl oz Baileys Irish Cream

Method

Pour in order then layer Baileys Irish Cream.

Technique: Shoot.

Comments: Baileys Irish Cream assures credibility and its softness will subtly inflict a powerful jab to wake you up and keep you on the hop!

Ready, Set, Go!

Ingredients

Glass: Tall Dutch Cordial

Mixers: 15mL/¹⁄₂fl oz Strawberry Liqueur
               15mL/¹⁄₂fl oz Banana Liqueur
               15mL/¹⁄₂fl oz Midori

Method

Layer in order and straw shoot.

Red Indian

Ingredients

Glass: Cordial (Lexington)

Mixers: 10mL/⅓fl oz Dark Crème de Cacao
10mL/⅓fl oz Peachtree Schnapps
15mL/½fl oz Canadian Club

Method

Layer in order.

Technique: Shoot.

Comments: Dark Crème de Cacao ripens the Peachtree to tantalise. CC takes the scalp!

Rusty Nail

Ingredients

Glass: Cordial (Embassy)

Mixers: 15mL/½fl oz Scotch Whisky

               15mL/½fl oz Drambuie

Method

Layer in order.

Technique: Shoot.

Comments: A pillow-softener, though this age-old blend will never cause fatigue. As a Shooter, great as "one for the road". The traditional cocktail is normally built over ice, in a 210mL/7oz Old Fashioned Spirit Glass.

Ryan's Rush

Ingredients

Glass: Cordial (Embassy)

Mixers: 10mL/⅓fl oz Kahlúa
10mL/⅓fl oz Baileys Irish Cream
10mL/⅓fl oz Rum

Method

Layer in order.

Technique: Shoot

Comments: An easy one. Don't be lulled by the pleasant taste, this one has a real kick.

Screaming Death Shooter

Ingredients

Glass: Tall Dutch Cordial

Mixers: 15mL/½fl oz Crème de Café Liqueur

              10mL/⅓fl oz Cougar Bourbon

              10mL/⅓fl oz DOM Benedictine

              5mL/⅙fl oz Bourbon

              5mL/⅙fl oz Bundaberg OP

Method

Layer in the above order. Lighting optional.

Technique: Shoot while flaming.

Comments: The pinnacle of endurance. Double layers of flammable fuel cushioned in ascending order by Crème de Café Liqueur, Bourbon and Benedictine, which sweetly numbs any pain. It's truth and dare.

Screwdriver Shooter

Ingredients

Glass: Whisky Shot

Mixers: 15mL/½fl oz Orange Liqueur

                    30mL/1½fl oz Vodka

Method

Layer in order.

Technique: Shoot.

Comments: Add a dash of Peachtree Schnapps and it's known as a "Fuzzy Navel". The Shooter mix departs from the traditional Screwdriver cocktail by the substitution of Orange Liqueur for Orange juice. The cocktail is also built over ice in a 210mL/7oz Old Fashioned Spirit glass.

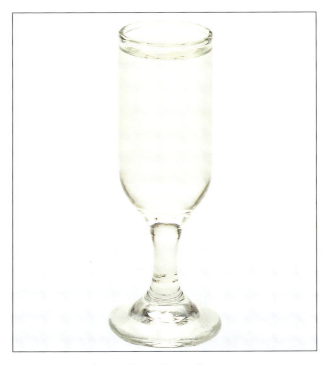

Sex in the Snow

Ingredients

Glass: Cordial (Lexington)

Mixers: 12mL/¹/₃fl oz Triple Sec Liqueur
12mL/¹/₃fl oz Malibu
12mL/¹/₃fl oz Ouzo

Method

Pour in order, then stir.

Technique: Straw Shoot.

Comments: the sub-zero temperature of this combination is chillingly refreshing when drunk through a straw.

Sherbert Burp

Ingredients

Glass: Tall Dutch Cordial

Mixers: 15mL/½fl oz Strawberry Liqueur
                30mL/1fl oz Champagne

Method

Pour Strawberry Liqueur then top up with Champagne.

Technique: Shoot.

Comments: Change the colour of your burp with any flavoured liqueur. Even better, multi-colour it!

Sidecar Shooter

Ingredients

Glass: Cordial (Lexington)

Mixers: 10mL/⅓fl oz Brandy
               15mL/½fl oz Cointreau*
               10mL/⅓fl oz Lemon Juice

Method

Layer Cointreau onto Brandy, float Lemon Juice, then optional to stir.

Technique: Shoot.

Comments: This old-fashioned, lemon-barley refreshment, filtered through Cointreau and lightly tanned with Brandy, restores your zest for life. A slightly different mix to the traditional Sidecar cocktail, which is shaken over ice and served in a 90mL/3oz Cocktail glass.

*Cointreau may be substituted with Triple Sec.

Silver Thread

Ingredients

Glass: Tall Dutch Cordial

Mixers: 15mL/½fl oz Creme de Menthe
              15mL/½fl oz Banana Liqueur
              15mL/½fl oz Tia Maria

Method

Layer in order.

Technique: Shoot or lick, sip and suck.

Comments: A great shooter to mend the fences. Try this one on with the oldies.

Slippery Nipple

Ingredients

Glass: Cordial (Embassy)

Mixers: 30mL/1fl oz Sambuca

15mL/½fl oz Baileys Irish Cream

Method

Layer in order.

Technique: Shoot

Comments: One of the originals, very well received. Cream floated on the Baileys becomes a **"Pregnant Slippery Nipple"**. Grand Marnier included makes a **"Slipadicthome"**.

Snake Bite

Ingredients

Glass: Cordial (Embassy)

Mixers: 20mL/²⁄₃fl oz Creme de Cafe Liqueur
10mL/¹⁄₃fl oz Green Chartreuse

Method

Layer in order, then light.

Technique: Straw shoot while flaming.

Comments: Score this shooter ten out of ten. Drink quickly or the straw will melt.

Spanish Fly

Ingredients

Glass: Whisky Shot

Mixers: 10mL/⅓fl oz Bianco Vermouth
                  15mL/½fl oz Tequila
                  20mL/⅔fl oz Whisky

Method

Build without ice.

Technique: Tandem.

Comments: No, it's not what you're twinkling eye and devious smirk assumes...it's better. A guaranteed survival capsule, capable of producing fantasies beyond those Spain is famous for.

Springbok

Ingredients

Glass: Cordial (Embassy)

Mixers: 20mL/²/₃fl oz Passionfruit Syrup
10mL/¹/₃fl oz Crème de Menthe Liqueur
5mL/¹/₆fl oz Ouzo

Method

Layer in order.

Technique: Shoot.

Comments: Named after the beautiful Springbok of Africa, a motif on the South African Rugby jersey.

Strawberry Cream

Ingredients

Glass: Cordial (Embassy)

Mixers: 20mL/²/₃fl oz Strawberry Liqueur
                 10mL/¹/₃fl oz Cream

Method

Layer in order.

Technique: Shoot.

Comments: begin your trip to the "World of Shooters" with this one. Cream acts as a buffer to entice the nervous and inexperienced. Strawberries calm what was needless concern.

Suction Cup

Ingredients

Glass: Cordial (Lexington)

Mixers: 20mL/²/₃fl oz Vodka

10mL/¹/₃fl oz Melon Liqueur

7mL/¹/₅fl oz Blue Curacao Liqueur

Method

Layer the Melon onto Vodka, then pour Blue Curacao.

Technique: Suction-straw shoot.

Comments: A supersonic vacuum results from this drinking method.

Suitor

Ingredients

Glass: Cordial (Lexington)

Mixers: 10mL/¹/₃fl oz Drambuie*
10mL/¹/₃fl oz Grand Marnier
10mL/¹/₃fl oz Baileys Irish Cream
7mL/¹/₅fl oz Milk

Method

Pour in order.

Technique: Shoot.

Comments: Milk inclusion coddles a cool moment, resettles anxieties when approaching the fair sex, guaranteed to excite romance.

*Drambuie may be substituted with Lochan Ora.

Sukiyaki

Ingredients

Glass: Cordial (Embassy)

Mixers: 10mL/¹⁄₃fl oz Mango Liqueur

                  10mL/¹⁄₃fl oz Apricot Brandy

                  10mL/¹⁄₃fl oz Malibu

Method

Layer in order.

Technique: Shoot.

Comments: Essential starter for s superb Japanese banquet.

Test Tube Baby

Ingredients

Glass: Tall Dutch Cordial

Mixers: 25mL/⁵/₆fl oz Grand Marnier
              20mL/²/₃fl oz Ouzo
              drop of Baileys Irish Cream

Method

Layer in order and shoot.

Technique: Shoot

Comments: Bubbles of refreshing Apricot guaranteed to get up your nose.

The Day After

Ingredients

Glass: Cordial (Embassy)

Mixers: 10mL/⅓fl oz Cointreau*
                    10mL/⅓fl oz Tequila
                    5 drops Blue Curacao Liqueur
                    10mL/⅓fl oz Green Chartreuse

Method

Layer Tequila onto Cointreau. Drop the Blue Curacao, then layer Green Chartreuse and light.

Technique: Shoot after flame extinguished.

Comments: An upside down day!

*Cointreau may be substituted with Triple Sec.

T.K.O.

Ingredients

Glass: Cordial (Embassy)

Mixers: 10mL/¹⁄₃fl oz Kahlúa

10mL/¹⁄₃fl oz Tequila

10mL/¹⁄₃fl oz Ouzo

Method

Layer in order.

Technique: Shoot.

Comments: Don't fall with this TKO, drink it with pleasure, recover without pain.

Tickled Pink

Ingredients

Glass: Whisky shot

Mixers: 40mL/1⅓fl oz White Crème de Menthe
                  5mL/⅙fl oz Grenadine Cordial

Method

Pour White Crème de Menthe followed by a dash of
Grenadine or Raspberry Cordial.

Technique: Shoot.

Comments: For those who are bashful when
complimented.

Towering Inferno

Ingredients

Glass: Cordial (Embassy)

Mixers: 10mL/¹/₃fl oz Dry Gin

               10mL/¹/₃fl oz Triple Sec Liqueur

               10mL/¹/₃fl oz Green Chartreuse

Method

Layer in order, then light.

Technique: Shoot while flaming.

Comments: Designed to set the night on fire.

Traffic Light

Ingredients

Glass: *Tall Dutch Cordial*

Mixers: *10mL/¹/₃fl oz Strawberry Liqueur*

             10mL/¹/₃fl oz Galliano

             25mL/⁵/₆fl oz Green Chartreuse

Method

Layer in order, light, then light.

Technique: *Suction-straw shoot.*

Comments: *Ready set go! Substitute Banana Liqueur for Galliano and Melon Liqueur for Green Chartreuse, for those with a sweet tooth.*

U-Turn

Ingredients

Glass: Whisky Shot

Mixers: 15mL/¹⁄₂fl oz Banana Liqueur
             30mL/1fl oz Tia Maria

Method

Layer in order.

Technique: Shoot.

Comments: The Banana offers the curve yet its Tia Maria that sends you around the bend. A complete change of direction.

Vibrator

Ingredients

Glass: Cordial (Embassy)

Mixers: 10mL/¹/₃fl oz Baileys Irish Cream

                  20mL/²/₃fl oz Southern Comfort

Method

Layer in order.

Technique: Shoot.

Comments: Batteries are not required for this stimulating and pulsating comfort.

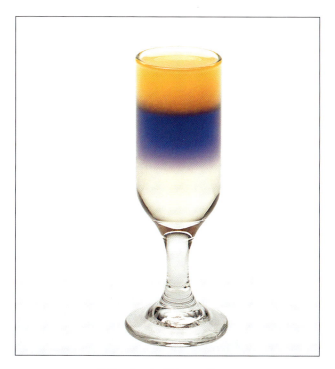

Violet Slumber

Ingredients

Glass: Cordial (Lexington)

Mixers: 15mL/½fl oz Malibu
10mL/⅓fl oz Parfait Amour
10mL/⅓fl oz Orange juice

Method

Layer in order.

Technique: Shoot.

Comments: Pretty to look at, better to drink, but don't slumber on this number.

Vodka-Tini

Ingredients

Glass: Cordial (Embassy)

Mixers: 25mL/⁵/₆fl oz Vodka

           5mL/¹/₆fl oz Dry Vermouth

Method

Pour in order, then stir.

Technique: Shoot.

Comments: No olive is required. Preferably served chilled.

Water-Bubba

Ingredients

Glass: Cordial (Lexington)

Mixers: 15mL/½fl oz Cherry Advocaat

10mL/⅓fl oz Advocaat

10mL/⅓fl oz Blue Curacao

Method

Pour Advocaat into Cherry Advocaat, then layer the Blue Curacao and shoot.

Technique: Shoot.

Comments: The Advocaat resembles an egg yolk, with veins of Cherry Advocaat. Also known as an **"Unborn Baby"**.

Andy Williams

Ingredients

Glass: 290mL/9oz Old Fashioned Glass

Mixers: 60mL/2fl oz Claytons Tonic
15mL/½fl oz Lime juice
dash sugar syrup
top-up with soda water

Method

Shake with ice and pour

Garnish: Thin lime slice floated in drink.

Comments: A delightful pre-dinner drink.

Andy's Passion

Ingredients

Glass: 270mL/9oz Hi-Ball Glass

Mixers: 90mL/3fl oz Passionfruit pulp
                  90mL/3fl oz Tropical juice
                  60mL/2fl oz Natural yoghurt

Method

Blend with ice and pour.

Garnish: Lime slice, swizzle stick and straw.

Comments: A taste of sunshine with the unique tang of passionfruit.

Apricot Smoothie

Ingredients

Glass: 390mL/12oz Poco Grande Glass

Mixers: 2 Apricots
90mL/3fl oz Milk
15mL/½fl oz Lemon juice
30mL/1fl oz Vanilla yoghurt

Method

Blend with ice and pour.

Garnish: Apricot slice and straws.

Comments: A large smooth drink, with apricot flavour.

Banana Bash

Ingredients

Glass: 310mL/10oz Hi-Ball Glass

Mixers: 1 ripe Banana
4 Raspberries
scoop Vanilla ice cream
90mL/3fl oz Tropical fruit juice

Method

Blend with ice and pour

Garnish: A sugar dusted raspberry on a banana wedge.

Comments: A great tasting blend of raspberry and banana.

Banana Berry Smoothy

Ingredients

Glass: 170mL/6oz Champagne Flute

Mixers: $^1/_3$ ripe Banana

60mL/2fl oz Orange juice

3 tablespoons Mixed berries

Method

Blend with ice and pour.

Garnish: Wedge banana and straw.

Comments: Berry bonanza.

Bell's Boomer

Ingredients

Glass: 470mL/16oz Fancy Hi-Ball Glass

Mixers: 30mL/1fl oz Apple juice

            30mL/1fl oz Orange juice

            30mL/1fl oz Grapefruit juice

            30mL/1fl oz Lime juice

            120mL/4fl oz dry ginger ale

Method

Build over Ice.

Garnish:

Comments: A large energising fruit drink, ideal before tackling those early morning breakers.

Blushing Berry

Ingredients

Glass: 260mL/8oz Margarita Glass

Mixers: 150mL/5fl oz milk
60mL/2fl oz raspberry cordial
60mL/2fl oz cream
15mL/½fl oz coconut milk
frozen raspberries

Method

Blend with ice, raspberry cordial, coconut milk, milk and whipped cream.

Garnish: Place frozen raspberries around rim.

Comments: Created by Mary Jane Porta of Termo, Albury and was a finalist in the Best Border Beverage Competition.

Bobby Dazzler

Ingredients

Glass: 290mL/9oz Poco Grande Glass

Mixers: 60mL/2fl oz Grenadine
              200mL/6fl oz Cola
              whipped cream
              hundreds and thousands

Method

Blend Grenadine with ice and pour.

Garnish: Pour into glass, top with whipped cream and sprinkle with hundreds and thousands. Place strawberry on side and serve with swizzle stick and straw.

Comments: By Maxine Nash, Bubbles-Wodonga Hotel, was a runner-up in the Best Border Beverage Competition.

Brazilian Breakdance

Ingredients

Glass: 390mL/12oz Poco Grande Glass

Mixers: 2 teaspoons Instant coffee

              Scoop Vanilla ice cream

              125mL/4fl oz Milk

Method

Blend with ice and pour.

Garnish: Teaspoon chocolate flakes.

Comments: A luscious, thick glass of iced coffee flavour, with just a hint of sweetness.

Candy Bar

Ingredients

Glass: 290mL/9oz Poco Grande Glass

Mixers: 200mL/6fl oz Milk
15mL/½fl oz Chocolate topping
30mL/1fl oz Caramel topping
whipped cream

Method

Blend with ice, milk chocolate and caramel topping.

Garnish: Top with whipped cream and sprinkle with icing sugar and shaved chocolate.

Comments: Created by Mary Ann Macure of Anthony's Restaurant, Wodonga and was a finalist in the Best Border Beverage Competition.

Cane Toad

Ingredients

Glass: 220mL/8oz Fancy Hi-Ball Glass

Mixers: 30mL/1fl oz Passionfruit pulp

30mL/1fl oz Sugar syrup

30mL/1fl oz Lemon juice

Top-up with Dry ginger ale

Method

Shake with ice and pour.

Garnish: Two lemon slices and mint leaves.

Comments: A fizzy cane toad without the poison, a very refreshing tarty drink.

Carrot Wizz

Ingredients

Glass: 200mL/6oz Old Fashioned Glass

Mixers: 60mL/2fl oz Tomato juice
½ medium carrot (thinly sliced)
dash horseradish sauce
dash Lemon juice

Method

Blend with ice and pour.

Garnish: Carrot top, floated on top.

Comments: "What's up Doc?" Created by Blaza Nikolic of the Hyatt Hotel, Melbourne.

Chocolate Frog

Ingredients

Glass: 390mL/12oz Poco Grande Glass

Mixers: 250mL/8fl oz Cola
15mL/½fl oz Chocolate topping
dash Peppermint essence
Whipping cream

Method

Build over ice.

Garnish: Top with whipped cream and sprinkle with nutmeg and place sliced strawberry on side of glass. Serve with swizzle stick and straw.

Comments: by Annie Brouwer of Thermo-Albury and was a runner-up in the Best Border Beverage Competition.

Claytons Sour

Ingredients

Glass: 200mL/6oz Bacchus Wine Glass

Mixers: 90mL/3fl oz Claytons Tonic

              15mL/½fl oz Sugar syrup

              60mL/2fl oz Lemon Juice

Method

Shake with ice and pour.

Garnish: Maraschino cherry.

Comments: Along the traditional lines.

Clover Blossom

Ingredients

Glass: 270mL/9oz Hi-Ball Glass

Mixers: 60mL/2fl oz Lemon Cordial
30mL/1fl oz Lime Juice
1 Egg White
dash Grenadine
Top-up with Tonic Water

Method

Blend with ice and pour.

Garnish: Lemon slice, mint leaf and straw.

Comments: A delicate fluffy concoction.

Cock-A-Doodle

Ingredients

Glass: 290mL/9oz Salud Grande Glass

Mixers: 90mL/3fl oz Dark grape juice

90mL/3fl oz Lemon juice

15mL/¹/₂fl oz Lime cordial

15mL/¹/₂fl oz Sugar syrup

dash Grenadine

Method

Shake with ice and strain.

Garnish: Lime slice and dark grapes on side of glass.

Comments: Wake up to this little refresher.

Coffee Crunch

Ingredients

Glass: 440mL/14oz Hurricane Glass

Mixers: 90mL/3fl oz Coconut cream
90mL/3fl oz Cream
1 egg
125mL/4fl oz iced coffee

Method

Blend with ice and pour.

Garnish: Sprinkle with cinnamon sugar, serve with straw and decorate as desired.

Comments: Created by Gaye Fendyke of Termo-Albury and was a runner-up in the Best Border Beverage Competition.

Corio Bay Sunset

Ingredients

Glass: 330mL/11oz Hi-Ball glass

Mixers: 4 Large Strawberries
30mL/1fl oz Lime juice
125mL/4fl oz Orange and mango juice
15mL/½fl oz Claytons Tonic
Top-up with Lemonade

Method

Blend with ice and strain.

Garnish: Orange slice.

Comments: A delightful combination of citrus and berry flavours.

Corra Bear

Ingredients

Glass: 290mL/10oz Poco Grande Glass

Mixers: 200mL/6fl oz Cola

30mL/1fl oz Iced coffee

Whipped cream

Method

Build over ice and stir.

Garnish: Top with whipped cream and place maraschino cherry on top, with a slice of kiwi fruit on side of glass. Serve with straws.

Comments: Created by Mary Jane Porta of Termo, Albury and was outright winner of the Best Border Beverages Competition.

Creamy Banana

Ingredients

Glass: 350mL/12oz Fiesta Grande Glass

Mixers: 1 ripe Banana, sliced
                30mL/1fl oz Coconut cream
                60mL/2fl oz Milk
                Scoop Vanilla ice cream

Method

Blend with ice and strain.

Garnish: Sprinkle with chocolate flakes.

Comments: A delicate creamy drink.

Dick Little

Ingredients

Glass: 350mL/12oz Fancy Hi-Ball Glass

Mixers;   60mL/2fl oz Apricot nectar

                    15mL/½fl oz Lime juice

                    Top-up with Bitter lemon

Method

Build over ice.

Garnish: Lemon slices on side of glass, swizzle stick and straw.

Doctor's Orders

Ingredients

Glass: 290mL/9oz Salud Grande Glass

Mixers: 30mL/1fl oz Lime juice

125mL/4fl oz Grapefruit juice

2 sachets Lite-n-Low

Top-up with Tonic Water

Method

Shake with ice and strain.

Garnish: Lime slice and straws.

Comments: A juice a day to keep the doctor away.

Fruit Mocquiri

Ingredients

Glass: 260mL/8oz Margarita Glass

Mixers: 60mL/2fl oz Strawberries, peaches or mango

15mL/½fl oz Sugar syrup

15mL/½fl oz Lemon juice

30mL/1fl oz Apple juice

Method

Blend with ice and pour.

Garnish: Small slice of the ingredient fruit.

Comments: A smooth rich blend of your favourite fruit. I particularly like mango, as used in the photograph above.

Fruit Squash

Ingredients

Glass: 330mL/10oz Hi-Ball Glass

Mixers: 2 Strawberries

4 Raspberries

Tablespoon crushed pineapple

Tablespoon Passionfruit pulp

$^1/_2$ Kiwi fruit

60mL/2fl oz Orange juice

Method

Blend with ice and pour.

Garnish: Berry studded pineapple spear.

Comments: A fruit lovers delight.

Gator

Ingredients

Glass: 170mL/6oz Champagne Flute

Mixers: 90mL/3fl oz Grapefruit juice

30mL/1fl oz Lime cordial

Method

Build over ice.

Garnish: Lime peel curl.

Comments: Sharp and tangy aperitif.

Fruit Squash

Ingredients

Glass: 330mL/10oz Hi-Ball Glass

Mixers: 2 Strawberries

4 Raspberries

Tablespoon crushed pineapple

Tablespoon Passionfruit pulp

$^1/_2$ Kiwi fruit

60mL/2fl oz Orange juice

Method

Blend with ice and pour.

Garnish: Berry studded pineapple spear.

Comments: A fruit lovers delight.

Health Farm

Ingredients

Glass: 270mL/9oz Hi-Ball Glass

Mixers: 90mL/3fl oz Pineapple juice
                    2 slices Cantaloupe melon
                    90mL/3fl oz Orange juice
                    2 teaspoons Honey
                    $^1/_2$ ripe Banana

Method

Blend with ice and pour.

Garnish: Cantaloupe wedge and swizzle stick.

Comments: A great drink for the health conscious. Created by Wayne Baker or Tousson Restaurant, Geelong.

Henry VIII

Ingredients

Glass: 210mL/7oz Old Fashioned Glass

Mixers: 60mL/2fl oz Apple juice

                    15mL/¹/₂fl oz Lemon juice

                    Top-up with Dry Ginger Ale

                    ¹/₂ teaspoon of Grenadine

Method

Build over ice.

Garnish: To finish, gently add Grenadine to top.

Comments: A very Piquant and gingery drink, suitable for afternoon relaxation.

Iron Man

Ingredients

Glass: 350mL/12oz Fancy Hi-Ball Glass

Mixers: 1 egg

45mL/1½fl oz Honey

1 ripe Banana, sliced

150mL/5fl oz Orange juice

Method

Blend with ice and pour.

Garnish: A vanilla bean floated, then sprinkle flake chocolate over top.

Comments: Choc-a-block with energy.

Created by Rowan Sapwell, Manager, Fishermen's Pier Restaurant Geelong.

Island Paradise

Ingredients

Glass: 90mL/3oz Martini Glass

Mixers: 30mL/1fl oz Orange juice

              15mL/¹⁄₂fl oz Coconut cream

              30mL/1fl oz Lime juice

              dash Sugar syrup

Method

Shake with ice and strain.

Garnish: Lime slice and sprig of mint.

Comments: Tropical tastes in a short and piquant quencher.

Issy Wassy

Ingredients

Glass: 230mL/8oz Hurricane Glass

Mixers: 125mL/4fl oz Milk
$^1/_2$ Banana
2 slices Cantaloupe melon

Method

Blend with ice and pour.

Garnish: Cantaloupe slice with straws.

Comments: For the smooth stylish chap.

Jaffa

Ingredients

Glass: 200mL/6oz Old Fashioned Glass

Mixers: scoop Chocolate Ice cream
                     90mL/3fl oz Orange juice

Method

Blend with ice and pour.

Garnish: 1 teaspoon grated chocolate on top.

Comments: Just like a liquid jaffa.

Jersey Cow

Ingredients

Glass: 290mL/9oz Old Fashioned Glass

Mixers: 180mL/6fl oz Cola

Scoop Chocolate Ice cream

Method

Stir over ice.

Garnish: Teaspoon of grated chocolate over top.

Comments: A choc-cola delight.

Jimmy's Beach Cruiser

Ingredients

Glass: 380mL/12oz Viva Grande Glass

Mixers: 6 Raspberries

2 tablespoons Crushed pineapple

60mL/2fl oz Orange juice

Top-up with Lemonade

Method

Blend with ice and pour.

Garnish: Two raspberries on side of glass, plus optional decoration.

Comments: A great blend of flavours.

Joh's Country

Ingredients

Glass: 350mL/12oz Fiesta Grande Glass

Mixers: 45mL/1½fl oz Pineapple juice
30mL/1fl oz Coconut cream
dash Lime Cordial
60mL/2fl oz Mango and Orange juice

Method

Blend with ice and pour.

Garnish: mango slice, straw and optional decoration.

Comments: Rich creamy coconut flavour.

Juice Combo

Ingredients

Glass: 270mL/8oz Footed Hi-Ball Glass

Mixers: 45mL/1½fl oz Pineapple juice
45mL/1½fl oz Orange juice
45mL/1½fl oz Apple juice
45mL/1½fl oz Dark grape juice
30mL/1fl oz Lime juice
15mL/½fl oz Sugar syrup

Method

Build over ice and stir.

Garnish: Two dark table grapes on side of glass.

Comments: A refreshing blend of juices.

Julie's Black Cat

Ingredients

Glass: 270mL/9oz Hi-Ball Glass

Mixers: 15mL/½fl oz Lemon juice
                    125mL/4fl oz Dark grape juice
                    60mL/2fl oz Lemonade
                    60mL/2fl oz Dry Ginger Ale

Method

Build over ice.

Garnish: Lemon twists dropped in glass, straw and optional decoration.

Comments: Let this one cross your path, a dry tasty drink.

Kate's Pink Echidna

Ingredients

Glass: 310mL/10oz Hi-Ball Glass

Mixers: 3 Strawberries

               2 slices Cantaloupe Melon

               30mL/1fl oz Sugar syrup

               dash Lemon juice

               Top-up with Lemonade

Method

Blend with ice and pour.

Garnish: Cantaloupe slice and small strawberry on side of glass.

Comments: A delicate melon flavour.

Lethal Weapon

Ingredients

Glass: 310mL/10oz Hi-Ball Glass

Mixers: 210mL/7fl oz V8 juice
1 teaspoon Chilli sauce
salt and pepper
15mL/½fl oz Lemon juice

Method

Build over ice and stir.

Garnish: Celery stalk.

Comments: Full of vitamins, but with a fiery bite at the end.
A great heart starter at breakfast time.

Mickey Mouse

Ingredients

Glass: 270mL/8oz Hi-Ball Glass

Mixers: 90mL/3fl oz Orange juice
                     30mL/1fl ozRaspberry cordial
                     90mL/3fl oz lemonade

Method

Build over ice.

Garnish: Two cherries on side of glass.

Comments: A dash of vitamin C for you sweet tooth.

Mintlup

Ingredients

Glass: 310mL/10oz Hi-Ball Glass

Mixers: large sprig of crushed mint

15mL/½fl oz Lime juice

90mL/3fl oz Dry Ginger ale

90mL/3fl oz Lemon & lime mineral water

Method

Build over ice.

Garnish: Mint leaf on lemon slice.

Comments: Southern hospitaly in prohibition days perhaps.

Mocktini

Ingredients

Glass: 90mL/3oz Martini Glass

Mixers: 15mL/1/2fl oz Lime juice
dash Lemon juice
60mL/2fl oz Tonic water

Method

Stir with ice and strain.

Garnish: A green olive on a toothpick or a lemon twist.

Comments: The classic cocktail, non-alcoholic version.

Mocquiri

Ingredients

Glass: 90mL/3oz Martini Glass

Mixers: 60mL/2fl oz Apple juice

15mL/1/2fl oz Lemon juice

15mL/1/2fl oz Sugar syrup

Method

Blend with Ice and strain

Garnish: Lemon or lime twist

Comments: An apple flavoured non-alcoholic Daiquiri.

Oramato

Ingredients

Glass: 240mL/8oz Footed Hi-Ball Glass

Mixers: 90mL/3fl oz Tomato juice

125mL/4fl oz Orange juice

Method

Shake with Ice and Pour

Garnish: Orange peel curl.

Comments: Try this orange tomato for a taste difference.

Peach Magic

Ingredients

Glass: 440mL/14oz Hurricane Glass

Mixers: 1 Peach or Apricot, stoned
90mL/3fl oz Orange and mango juice
90mL/3fl oz Apple juice
top-up with Dry Ginger Ale

Method

Build over ice and pour.

Garnish: Watermelon slice and stemmed maraschino cherry.

Comments: A large refreshing taste of the orchard.

Pina Con Nada

Ingredients

Glass: 270mL/9oz Footed Hi-Ball Glass

Mixers: 90mL/3fl oz Pineapple juice

30mL/1fl oz Coconut cream

15mL/½fl oz Sugar syrup

Method

Blend with ice and pour.

Garnish: Wedge of pineapple and a strawberry with straws.

Comments: The creamy non-alcoholic version of the famous Pina Colada.

Shirley Temple

Ingredients

Glass: 310mL/10oz Hi-Ball Glass

Mixers: 15mL/½fl oz Grenadine

ginger ale or lemonade to top-up

Method

Build over ice.

Garnish: Slice of orange, serve with swizzle stick and two straws.

Comments: For a tangy variation to this drink try a Shirley Temple No.2. Use the following: 60ml pineapple juice to a glass half full of ice. Top with lemonade, float 15ml passionfruit pulp on top and garnish with pineapple wedge and cherry.

Shrinking Violet

Ingredients

Glass:	270mL/9oz Hi-Ball Glass
Mixers:	125mL/4fl oz Dark Grape juice
	90mL/3fl oz Lemonade
	15mL/½fl oz Lime juice

Method

Build with ice and stir.

Garnish: Two dark grapes and straw.

Comments: A light but sharp drink.

Spazz

Ingredients

Glass: 310mL/10oz Hi-Ball Glass

Mixers: ¹/₂ Peach or Apricot, stoned

150mL/5fl oz Pineapple juice

15mL/¹/₂fl oz Lime juice

Method

Blend with ice and pour.

Garnish: Pour a teaspoon Grenadine over top of drink, add apricot slice and straw.

Comments: A long, delicately flavoured drink.

Strawberry Zappie

Ingredients

Glass: 310mL/10oz Hi-Ball Glass

Mixers: 4 strawberries
180mL/6fl oz Apple juice
30mL/1fl oz lemon juice
dash lime cordial

Method

Blend with ice and pour.

Garnish: Small strawberry on straw.

Comments: A sharp, tasty, refresher.

Sundowner

Ingredients

Glass: 210mL/7ozOld Fashion Glass

Mixers: 75mL/2½fl oz Orange Juice and mango juice
15mL/½fl oz Lemon juice
45mL/1½fl oz Clayton's Tonic

Method

Shake with ice and pour.

Garnish: Lemon slice, floated

Comment: A citrus tang to activate the taste buds.

Sydneysider

Ingredients

Glass: 350mL/12oz Fiesta Grande Glass

Mixers: 30mL/1fl oz Lemon juice
30mL/1fl oz Orange juice
30mL/1fl oz Grapefruit juice
30mL/1fl oz Pineapple juice
60mL/2fl oz Apple juice
½ Egg white
dash Grenadine

Method

Shake with ice and pour.

Garnish: Apple fan.

Comments: Fruit medley in the Opera House.
Created by Anthony Carroll of The Fresh Ketch Restaurant.

Virgin Maria

Ingredients

Glass: 270mL/8oz Footed Hi-Ball Glass

Mixers: 180mL/6fl oz Tomato juice
dash Lemon juice
15mL/½fl oz chilli sauce

Method

Blend with ice and pour.

Garnish: Cucumber slice, cherry tomatoes and optional decoration.

Comments: A very hot and spicy drink, guaranteed to keep you that way.

Virgin Mary

Ingredients

Glass: 270mL/8oz Hi-Ball Glass

Mixers: 150mL/5fl oz Tomato juice

15mL/¹/₂fl oz Lemon juice

teaspoon Worcestershire sauce

2 or 3 drops Tabasco sauce

Salt and pepper to taste

Method

Build over ice and stir.

Garnish: Celery stalk, lemon slice and straws.

Comments: A spicy refreshing start to the day.

Index

Cocktail index

Index

Index

Shooters index

Index

Index

Non alcoholic index